SAMY TANAGHO

THE **L** TRUE
O
V
E

COPYRIGHT

DEDICATION

I dedicate this book to my neighbors, coworkers,
and all the precious people I meet and love.

TABLE OF CONTENTS

God Is in Love With You

God loves you so much that He wants to embrace you as a father embraces his child. Yes, God wants you to become His child. He wants to have a close relationship with you based upon mutual love. God created you to enjoy a joyful, unbroken fellowship with Him forever.

God does not desire that your relationship with Him consist of religious rituals and traditions. He wants you to know Him through a personal relationship and to experience His love, forgiveness, and divine presence and guidance.

God has a wonderful plan for your life. He designed you in such a way that you will never be completely satisfied and happy without experiencing His perfect will and presence. God desires to fill your life with joy, love, peace, and hope.

A Letter for You

Dear Friend,

Everyone searches for love; but for many, it proves elusive. The Beatles sang, "All You Need Is Love" and then they disbanded! Many couples think they have found love, but then it slips away from them. They wonder if what they had was true love after all. I want to tell you about an unconditional love that will revolutionize your life. In fact, it is the greatest love story in human history; it is God's love for you!

The most prevalent characteristic revealed about God in the Bible is that He is a loving God. Love is not just one of God's glorious attributes; love is the essence of God's being.

Since February 1976, I have personally experienced God's deep love. I have also met thousands who have had—and still have—the same experience. The Bible says, "We know and rely on the love God has for us. God is love" (1 John 4:16).

My dear reader, it is not by accident you are reading this book right now. It is a divine appointment designed by the relational God to draw you toward Him so that you can know Him. God is passionate in His love for you and invites you to discover the depth of that love.

Warmly,

Sam Tanagh

1

❧

God Loved You
When He Created You

There is one and only one living God. He is infinite, eternal, Personal Spirit who created human beings. It has been known for a long time that a blind force could never produce your intellect, sensibility, will, emotions, and conscience:

> You made all the delicate, inner parts of my body and knit me together in my mother's womb. Thank You for making me so wonderfully complex. Your workmanship is marvelous (Psalm 139:13-14).

GOD IS THE ARCHITECT OF YOUR BODY

Dear reader, please ask any physician how wonderfully complex the human body is, such as the eye or the brain. This is because you are custom-designed by the Creator, God. In the darkness of your mother's belly, God shaped you and caused you to grow. You will never be duplicated. There is no other person that has your fingerprints. God created only one of you.

God said, "I knew you before I formed you in your mother's womb" (Jeremiah 1:5). You were not born by accident. You were created by the awesome, almighty God who knows all the details of your life. God told us, "The very hairs on your head are all numbered" (Matthew 10:30).

Since God created you, He knows how to make you satisfied and happy. He deserves your attention because He is your Maker.

God said, "I have cared for you since you were born. Yes, I carried you before you were born. I will be your God throughout your lifetime until your hair is white with age. I made you and I will care for you. I will carry you along and save you" (Isaiah 46:3-4).

CHAPTER

2

❦

God Loved You
When He Created the Universe

In the beginning God created the heavens and the earth.

- Genesis 1:1

To say that you and this universe exist by chance is like saying a bunch of strings, drums, and sticks composed a beautiful symphony. The truth is that intelligent beings compose symphonies and they own what they create. The Bible also agrees with this right of ownership: "The earth is the Lord's, and everything in it. The world and all its people belong to him" (Psalm 24:1).

God created animals, birds, fish, colorful leaves, and flowers. God made fertile soil, the complex system of the chemical structure of the earth. God also created the ground-producing food that your body needs and enjoys: herbs, vegetables, and fruits. Snow, rain, and water fall down from heaven to provide rivers. God gave us oceans, light, air, and oxygen-nitrogen gaseous mixtures. We don't find these blessings on any other planet.

> Sing out your thanks to the Lord, sing praises to our God with a harp. He covers the heavens with clouds, provides rain for the earth (Psalm 147:7-8).

Have you also considered the sunshine? The earth exists 93 million miles away from the sun. If the earth were any closer, we would burn. If the earth were a little farther away from the sun, we would freeze. God gave us the perfect temperature for living. Furthermore, the moon is precisely located in the correct place from the earth.

One must exercise blind faith to accept the evolution theory. Since pigs don't produce lambs and dogs don't produce kittens, it appears that each species produces its own kind. Fish produce fish and humans produce humans; humans can't come from any other species. An explosion has never created order. A big bang could never produce a sunset or a rose—only chaos.

When we look at the magnificent universe we live in, we realize that God gave all people enough evidence to show them that there is a supreme, intelligent, good

Designer who called into existence the physical universe and He keeps the universe in perfect order.

Do you agree that every building must have a builder? If so, then creation absolutely proves that there is a creator. Nothing can't cause everything to exist in harmony:

> The heavens proclaim the glory of God. The skies display His craftsmanship. Day after day they continue to speak; night after night they make Him known (Psalm 19:1-2).

Precious reader, you may enjoy the created things of this world, but they will never give you complete rest or deep satisfaction because you were made to have a personal relationship with The Creator of this world, your one and only Maker.

3

❧

Wherever You Are, God Loves You

In spite of any intentional or unintentional mistakes you have made, God is greater than a person's foolishness, weaknesses, failures, sins, hang-ups, or regrets. Even if you are doing wrong right now, such as lying, stealing, cheating, using drugs, or living an immoral lifestyle, God wants you to know that He will not give up on you. If you feel shameful as a result of a failure, your failure is not greater than God's power to give you success.

God still loves you and desires to forgive you. He wants to embrace you and cover you with His love, grace, and favor. He wants to give you a new life, a fresh start, and set your feet in the right direction.

O Lord, You are so good, so ready to forgive, so full of unfailing love for all who ask for Your help (Psalm 86:5).

My friend, please consider the heart God has for you. The following passage presents a glimpse of His love. Jesus said,

What do you think? If a man owns a hundred sheep, and one of them wanders away, will he not leave the ninety-nine (secure sheep) on the hills and go to look for the one that has wandered off? And if he finds it, I tell you the truth, he is happier about that one (lost) sheep than about the ninety-nine that did not wander off. In the same way your Father in heaven is not willing that any . . . should be lost (Matthew 18:12-14).

Jesus tells this story to help us understand that when we are lost, God will relentlessly pursue us because He cares for us.

WHERE ARE YOU?

Do you feel hurt, confused, or bitter? Let me assure you that God desires to set you free from these negative feelings and give you rest. He also desires to remove any guilty feelings you have from wrong decisions you may have made. God will help you overcome all of your negative habits.

If you have become poor or lonely; if your life doesn't look so good because of your mistakes or circumstances; if the people closest to you, even religious people and leaders, let you down—call out to God. He will never disappoint you. God said,

> Can a mother forget her nursing child? Can she feel no love for the child she has borne? But even if that were possible, I would not forget you! See, I have written your name on the palms of My hands (Isaiah 49:15-16).

I am not sure what is bothering you. Your life may be full of negative circumstances. You may have health issues or other personal problems that frustrate, disappoint, and overwhelm you. Maybe you have a financial crisis and you are barely able to keep your head above water.

Others of you might believe you don't have any serious problems. You may feel you are a smart, strong survivor who has accomplished a lot. Yet, in spite of your achievements, you feel restless and incomplete. Sometimes you feel like screaming or crying. You're not sure exactly what you can do to be happy.

Do any of these scenarios describe your life situation? As a matter of fact, every living person will face problems and sometimes tragedies.

GOD'S PROMISE TO YOU

Listen. God is speaking to you: "When you go through deep waters, I will be with you. When you go through rivers of difficulty, you will not drown. When you walk through the fire of oppression, you will not be burned up. The flames will not consume you. For I am the Lord, your God…your Savior" (Isaiah 43:2-3).

All of your crises, problems, and challenges do not surprise God. They are not impossible for Him to solve. Your enemies may have a harsh grip upon you, but it is not stronger than God's power to deliver you.

If you are in a deep hole, God will get you out of it. No matter how low you are, God's hand is able to lift you up to a high place. "With God everything is possible" (Matthew 19:26). God is the most powerful person who understands you and loves you the most. He is the most qualified person to help you. As you communicate and talk with God, you will discover His wonderful thoughts about you. God will take away all the fears that exist within you and He will fill your mind with peace and a living hope.

God will take you from where you are right now to a wonderful place where He created you to be. You will then discover that this is the best place for you. You can count on God's awesome wisdom, His good character and nature. Relax and fully surrender your life to God.

Trust His power to transform your life to be the best you can ever be.

Give all your worries and cares to God, for He cares about you (1 Peter 5:7).

God will calm the storms you are facing. He will enable you to ride above the wild waves that are striking at your life because when God is working in your life, problems are no longer dominant. God's passionate love for you and His almighty power working on your behalf will overpower everything that is against you. God wants to be your Hero. Will you let Him?

God will answer your prayers, solve your problems, or help you deal with them successfully and fill your inner being with His love and joy. He will help you cope with difficult situations and difficult people and will give you the power and wisdom to enjoy the future. William Carey, a Christian leader, once said, "The future is as bright as the promises of God."

It is important for you to discover that God sent Jesus to reveal to us the most satisfying and thrilling life we can live on earth. Jesus said,

My purpose is to give them a rich and satisfying life (John 10:10).

God sent Jesus to make it possible for us to enjoy eternal life with Him. Jesus said, "Most assuredly, I say to you, he who believes in Me has everlasting life" (John 6:47).

Throughout this book, I explain in a simple way how, even now, you can be sure you are going to heaven when you die. God will set you free even from the fear of death.

Because we are more than a body, we have a soul and spirit. One day your body will die and your life here on earth will end, but your soul and spirit will continue to live forever.

I am sure you agree with me that we cannot be completely happy here on earth (now) unless we know for sure that we will enjoy happiness throughout eternity. Likewise, if someone put us on an airplane and told us to have a good time, we could not really enjoy our journey if we did not know where we were going. But if we knew we were headed to Hawaii, the time in the airplane would be exciting and enjoyable.

EVEN THOUGH YOU DON'T LOVE HIM . . .

God wants you to know that His eyes are always upon you—you are always on His mind. God loves you infinitely. We read in His Word,

> How precious are your thoughts about me, Oh God. They cannot be numbered! I can't even count them, they outnumber the grains of sand! And when I wake up, You are still with me! (Psalm 139:17-18).

You might be thinking, *But I don't love God.* Let me reply. God is aware of everything; all the details of your life. God sees and knows you—yet still loves you. Even if you are against God, God is seeking to melt the harshness of your heart by His persistent love. God said, "Yes, I have loved you with an everlasting love; therefore with lovingkindness I have drawn you" (Jeremiah 31:3).

The most important Person in the universe thinks about you, seeks your well-being, and desires to have a love relationship with you. Will you accept God's offer? Please, don't think of this as strange. If you are a parent, you also desire that your children love you, and you reward them when they love you. God rewards those who love Him.

God's reward to you when you love Him is beyond your wildest dream. God promised, "No eye has seen, no ear has heard, and no mind has imagined what God has prepared for those who love Him" (1 Corinthians 2:9).

Even though you ignored God most of the time, you didn't care about knowing Him or knowing His Word, with open arms He waits for you. God's love toward you is steadfast and stable forever. You can start enjoying His love when you start talking to Him, reading His Word, and receiving what He has for you.

God will always respect your desire and give you the freedom to choose or reject Him. However, God will continue to persuade you to choose and trust Him and walk with Him because He knows that this is the only pathway to your happiness.

After you choose God, even if you changed your mind, hardened your heart, ignored Him, and strayed far from Him, God will seek to bring you back to a love relationship with Him. You might ask how I know that. Well, now you are making me confess a past I am not proud of.

MY PAST LIFE

Although I experienced God's love in my heart and tasted the good life He has for me, I was unfaithful to Him—not only once, but so many times. Even so, God sought me every time I forgot about Him and persuaded me to return to Him. God's Word is true, "If we are unfaithful, He remains faithful, for He cannot deny who He is" (2 Timothy 2:13). I regretted every time I turned my back on God because I couldn't enjoy my personal relationship with Him or His blessings.

This is what happened. I was in law school in my homeland in Cairo, Egypt. On February 17, 1976, I believed that Jesus died on the cross to pay the penalty for everything I did wrong. At that time, I felt God so close to me—I enjoyed His love, forgiveness, and presence. Singing with joy, I felt like I was His child.

Then I started working as a defense lawyer in my father's prestigious law firm. Most of my clients were drug dealers and all of them were guilty.

I wanted to make my father proud of me and become a successful lawyer like him and my grandfather. So do you know what I did to get my clients out of prison? I made the guilty innocent. I disobeyed God. Not only did I lie to get ahead, I tried to silence my conscience as much as I could by using the best kind of illegal drugs, like hash (similar to marijuana). At the same time, I would drive to the Suez Canal, look at the water in the Red Sea, listen to Christian songs, and just cry. I knew better than to live this way, but I did. Even in this rebellious lifestyle, God gently spoke to me and He did not let me go.

After a couple of years struggling with my desires to get what the world offers, such as money, fame, prestige, and illicit drug use, God won. He talked to me in many ways but especially through the Bible. In Hebrews chapter 11, I read that Moses was born and raised to be a prince in Egypt but he chose to leave Egypt. He preferred to suffer doing God's will rather than stay in Egypt and enjoy the pleasures of sin. God persuaded me to leave my sinful life in Egypt. He never talked to me in an audible voice, but I knew it was God.

When I told my parents of my decision to leave Egypt, they cried. Later, my father wrote that this was the hardest time in his life. In 1980, I left my beloved parents, brothers, sisters, legal career, and properties and went to America. I placed my faith in God and in His Word to take care of me.

Living in America was tough. I didn't understand English nor the culture. For instance, sometimes when I saw a beautiful girl in the church, I would ask her for her parent's phone number. She would always ask, "Why?"

I told her, "I would like my parents to call your parents."

She would again ask, "Why?"

"So our families can pray and talk about the possibility of us getting married."

After many rejections, I discovered that this is not a cool way to approach an American girl even though it's the most honorable way in my culture.

When I first arrived in America, I worked as a food server for many years while studying for the California Bar Exam. But God did not guide me to be a lawyer. He did not want me to have a demanding career. Instead, He wanted me to focus on serving Him. Most of my family thought I was not successful because I wasn't rich like them.

In spite of my lack of resources and abilities, all the foolish mistakes I made, all my weaknesses, sins, and failures, God was with me. He never let go of my hand, even when I let go of His. As I realized His care and love for me, I did my best to have a good relationship with Him. I was not perfect; but every time I fell down, I asked Him to help me get up again, to continue to believe in Him and His Word, and to walk with Him.

Throughout the years, God protected me from danger, death, evil people, harm—even from myself and my wrong inclinations. God used many wonderful Christian teachers to help me grow and mature in my relationship with Him.

One evening, I was so tired from working as a waiter and discouraged from my negative circumstances, I just cried and asked God to encourage me. That night, my pastor taught from the Bible about the life of Joseph—how Joseph walked faithfully with God and God made him a successful man in spite of all the difficult circumstances he faced.

GOD'S WORD IS TRUE

True to His promises, God guided me to get a simple job in the American government and provided for me. He has blessed me with a wonderful wife who loves me deeply. God is my most loyal friend.

Before the tragedy of 9/11, God led me to write a book in English entitled *Glad News! God Loves You, My Muslim Friend.* This book presents biblical teachings to Muslims in the most understandable way and answers their questions about the Christian faith. Since 9/11, the book has been published in many languages and distributed internationally.

For more than ten years, I have been traveling all over the United States and many parts of the world for speaking engagements. I have gone to Hawaii with my wife a few times where not only did I get to speak in churches but Christian brothers and sisters showed us beautiful beaches and other beautiful scenery every day and gave us their houses and cars to use.

I enjoy the new life God has given me. I even forgot the pain of negative memories. I could never be satisfied and happy in life without knowing God, discovering and following His Word, and experiencing His guidance and will. Now I have a good relationship with Him. I know God much better and I appreciate Him so deeply. I have a strong faith in Him and His Word.

But enough about me.

LOOKING FOR SATISFACTION

God didn't create us just to exist, to acquire lots of stuff, or to accomplish a lot of tasks. Often people think, "If I could just get that job or marry that person, I will be so happy." But when they reach their goal, they discover they want something else. The truth is we were created for something much bigger than ourselves, way deeper and more significant than our ideas.

When you take a deeper look at your life now, you know that something important is missing. You also know that you were born to have and enjoy more than you do right now. What is this missing joy? Simply put, it's having the right relationship with your Creator.

When God's love permeates your life—when you experience it through everyday circumstances and feel it within you—you will become a different person. God's persistent love will capture your mind and heart.

Keep reading and you will be thrilled to discover what God wants to give you.

YOU WILL BE THRILLED WHEN YOU TRUST GOD

God not only promises to help you meet your responsibilities, He wants you to enjoy living. God desires to lavish on you so many gifts and blessings as you walk with Him.

Whatever is good and perfect comes down to us from God, our Father (James 1:17).

Receiving and enjoying God's blessings can be limited only by you, not by His desire or ability to give them to you. We read in the Bible that "without faith it is impossible to please Him, for he who comes to God must believe that He is, and that He is a rewarder of those who diligently seek Him" (Hebrews 11:6).

God desires to fill your life with His beauty. He then asks you to allow Him to display His beauty through you—through your smile, your spirit, your actions, and your words. When you plug into God's plan for your life, you will discover that it is perfect. God said, "For I know the plans I have for you, they are plans for good and not for disaster, to give you a future and a hope" (Jeremiah 29:11).

As you grow in your relationship with God, you will discover that He gave you many talents and gifts. As you believe in God and His Word, you will be in harmony with His plan. You will experience a partnership with God to accomplish many of His eternal purposes as He has destined you to achieve great things.

> Now all glory to God, who is able through His mighty power at work within us, to accomplish infinitely more than we might ask or think (Ephesians 3:20).

The more you choose God and trust Him, the more you will experience the awesome things God wants to do for you, in you, and through your life. As a result, you will enjoy living the most exciting, adventurous, significant, and meaningful life you can ever have. Also, your friendship with God will grow closer. God promised you in the Bible "come close to God, and God will come close to you" (James 4:8).

And when your life on earth ends, God will reward you generously throughout eternity. To be on God's side is to be on the winning side. He guarantees it. We read, "The Lord was with Joseph, so he succeeded in everything he did" (Genesis 39:2).

As you continue reading this book, you will discover more of God's mind and heart. The more you read, the more you are expressing your desire to have a better relationship with God. One of the greatest American presidents, Abraham Lincoln, said, "I believe the Bible is the best gift God has ever given to man." Our great God says to you,

> I will guide you along the best pathway for your life.
> I will advise you and watch over you (Psalm 32:8).

4

❦

God Loves You.
He Gave You His Word

Do you know that every year the Bible is the best selling book in the world?

> Your Word is a lamp to guide my feet and a light for my path (Psalm 119:105).

I believe that after reading this book, you will say,

> I rejoice in Your Word like one who discovers a great treasure (Psalm 119:162).

I can try to convince you that the ice cream cake I'm eating is delicious, but you will never really know until you taste it for yourself. In a similar way, you will discover and enjoy your best life when you open your heart and mind while reading the truths that God desires to reveal to you in this book:

> Taste and see that the Lord is good. Oh, the joys of those who take refuge in Him (Psalm 34:8).

God gave us His Word so we can enjoy the best life possible here on earth and so we can forever enjoy His presence and pleasures in His kingdom.

THE LIVING REVELATION OF GOD

We know from reading the Bible that Jesus Christ is the perfect revelation of God to the human race and that Jesus announced the good news of God's love and salvation. Then he commanded his disciples to share this good news with all people (Matthew 28:18-20).

FOUR PRESENTATIONS OF THE ONE GOSPEL

Four of Jesus' disciples recorded the words and accounts of His life on earth. God knew that if we had only one account of the life of Jesus, many people would be suspicious and wonder if that one account were true. But God gave us four accounts written by four separate disciples—Matthew, Mark, Luke, and John.

Matthew and John were eyewitnesses; they were two of Jesus' twelve disciples. Luke, a historian (Luke 1:1-4), received his information from eyewitnesses (Luke 1:2). Mark spent extensive time with Peter, one of Jesus' closest friends who witnessed all of the major events in His life.

These four followers of Christ wrote testimonies of Jesus' life and teachings. Each writer simply tells the story in a different way.

Jesus assured the Gospel writers that the Holy Spirit would guide their writings and remind them of what He had spoken: "The Helper, the Holy Spirit, whom the Father will send in My name, He will teach you all things, and bring to your remembrance all things that I said to you" (John 14:26).

The Bible describes God as an infinite Spirit. He is One and His oneness is compound. Within the Divine Unity, there are three eternal persons of one divine nature who share the same self-existing essence; they are called the Father, the Son (Jesus), and the Holy Spirit.

So my dear reader, when you read the Gospel as recorded by John, you are reading the Word of God as taught by Jesus and written by John, who was inspired by the Holy Spirit. John was a close companion of Jesus and an eyewitness to his death, resurrection, and ascension, as were Matthew and nine other disciples.

The apostle John assures us that the disciples actually walked and talked with Jesus:

> We proclaim to you the one who existed from the beginning [Jesus], whom we have heard and seen. We saw him with our own eyes and touched him

with our own hands. He is the Word of Life. This one who is life itself was revealed to us, and we have seen him. And now we testify and proclaim to you (1 John 1:1-2).

They wrote one message—the gospel of Jesus Christ. God's love for you and me and for all people is revealed in the gospel.

The entire New Testament contains the Word of God which will guide you to enjoy your life here on earth and live happily forever.

OTHER NEW TESTAMENT WRITINGS

In addition to the four presentations of the Gospel, the New Testament also contains inspired teachings and letters written by apostles and disciples of Jesus to different groups of Christians, and ultimately, to all believers. As the apostle Paul said, "For I pass on to you what I received from the Lord himself" (1 Corinthians 11:23). (See also 1 Thessalonians 2:13.)

All the words written in the New Testament are significant echoes of Jesus' teachings. They help us to grow morally and spiritually and to discover God's wonderful plan for our lives. The four presentations of the Gospel, along with the other writings of the New Testament, are interdependent.

For example, Peter declared, "For we did not follow cleverly invented stories when we told you about the power and coming of our Lord Jesus Christ, but we were eyewitnesses of His majesty" (2 Peter 1:16).

The apostles repeatedly challenged people living at that time to question any of the hundreds of eyewitnesses for verification of the life, death, resurrection, and teachings of Jesus. (See Acts 2:22-24; 5:30-32; 26:25-26.)

The whole New Testament was written soon after Jesus' death (AD 40-96).

DIVINE INSPIRATION COMES FROM GOD

"All Scripture is inspired by God and is useful to teach us what is true" (2 Timothy 3:16). This verse means God is the ultimate Author of the message in the Bible.

My friend, the most important proof that the Bible is the divine Word of God is when you read it; then you will see and understand the full, true picture of life, people, and yourself. You will receive answers to what life is all about and what you believe in your heart will make sense in your mind.

As you are reading the Bible and seeking God, God will speak to you. The more you ask God to help you do the right thing, God will draw closer to you.

When I was very young, I wanted to draw near to important people. I even dreamt that I and the president of my country, Egypt, became good friends. Wow, can you imagine how awesome you will feel when you know that God is your friend?

Jesus said, "Those who accept my Commandments and obey them are the ones who love me. And because they love me . . . I will reveal myself to each of them" (John 14:21).

God will personally guide you to discover Him and live the most satisfying life He created for you to enjoy.

THE CERTAINTY OF THE BIBLE

The word "Bible" is taken from the Greek word *biblia*, which means "book." The Bible is divided into two parts, the Old Testament and the New Testament. The word "testament" means "covenant," which refers to the relationship between God and His people. The Old Testament contains the Torah, the Psalms, and the books of the prophets.

There are hundreds of books presenting conclusive evidence that demonstrates the authenticity and reliability of the Bible. One popular book on this topic is *The New Evidence that Demands a Verdict* by Josh McDowell.[1]

You may be asking, "How do I know with certainty that any writing is from God?" Test it. The Bible exhorts its readers to "test everything that is said. Hold onto what is good" (1 Thessalonians 5:21).

God has given us minds to test such things. So what kind of test is there to see if something is supernaturally inspired by God? There are two:

TEST #1 - ARE BIBLICAL PROPHECIES ACCURATE?

The Bible contains a great number of specific, historical prophecies that have been accurately fulfilled.

In the Bible, God declares that He is outside of time: "I am God, and there is no other; I am God, and there is none like Me. I make known the end from the beginning, from ancient times, what is still to come" (Isaiah 46:9-10).

To test any supposed holy book, the first consideration should be to find proof. Are words proof? Of course not, for any word can be alleged to be true. Is belief proof? Of course not. People can be taught to believe something that isn't true.

However, if someone could always foretell the future with total accuracy—if the specific predictions are always fulfilled and historically verifiable—it would establish that the information came from God. Only God possesses the ability to fully know what is to come.

Throughout this book, you will discover some of the many, amazing, specific prophecies in the Old Testament concerning Jesus' birth, life, ministry, crucifixion, death, and resurrection. These prophecies were written hundreds of years before Jesus' birth. Each one was fulfilled with one hundred percent accuracy in the life of Christ.

Scientific Prophecies:

Another form of prophecy is the scientific information found in the Bible. These facts were given to biblical authors 2,000 years or more before modern science discovered them. For example, the Bible records that the earth is round (Isaiah 40:22). And "God hangs the earth on nothing" (Job 26:7). Today, we know these are facts.

In his book, *Science and the Bible,* Dr. Henry Morris identifies many of the scientific prophecies found in the Bible regarding biology, hydrology, geology, etc. and how they correlate with scientific facts known today.[2]

Many religious leaders have claimed that their message come from God, but none of their words have become fulfilled prophecies. Only the Bible passes this test. Its detailed, fulfilled, historical prophecies provide evidence for its authenticity without a doubt. If you would like to learn more about biblical prophecy, another excellent reference is *Every Prophecy of the Bible* by John F. Walvoord.[3]

TEST #2 - IS THE BIBLE RELIABLE?

The evidence for reliability of the biblical manuscripts far exceeds the evidence for all other ancient writings. Biblical researchers, Geisler and Nix, conclude, "In contrast to the total number of over 5,000 New Testament manuscripts known today, other religious and historical books of the ancient world pale in significance." More detailed evidence can be found in two classical books: *From God to Us: How We Got Our Bible* by Norman Geisler[4] and William Nix and *The New Testament Documents: Are They Reliable?* by F. F. Bruce.[5]

The Septuagint

The Septuagint is the Greek translation of the Hebrew Old Testament. This version was written around 270 BC and is well documented in both Jewish and secular history. BC means "before Christ," indicating that a date is before the Christian era. The content shows consistent accuracy with today's Old Testament and verifies all the prophecies of the coming of Jesus Christ (Messiah) that were translated from Hebrew into Greek almost three hundred years before Christ was born!

Archeology

Archaeology also affirms the accuracy of the Bible. In 1974, *Time Magazine* published an article that stated,

> After more than two centuries of facing the heaviest scientific guns that could be brought to bear, the Bible has survived, and is perhaps better for the siege. Even on the critic's own terms—historical fact—the Scriptures seem more acceptable now than when the rationalists began the attack.

Archaeological findings by both Christians and non-Christians have confirmed the reliability and the accuracy of the biblical writers regarding numerous customs, names, places, and events. (See *Halley's Bible Handbook).*[6]

Only the Bible amazingly predicts precise historical events centuries in advance of their fulfillment. These prophecies are supported by archaeological evidence.

These prophecies were revealed by God who is eternal. He has no beginning nor end. He created time and subjects man to it. But God exists outside of time and knows all things.

As you continue to read this book, you will discover how awesome God is. I pray that you will also experience some of the wonderful life God desires you to have.

5

God's Sacrificial Love Is His Response
to the Wrong We Have Done

People know right from wrong; they have a sense of morality. The conscience that God gave them acts as the voice of God in their soul (Romans 2:14-15).

For instance, everyone knows that it is wrong to lie, steal, murder, and hurt someone emotionally or physically. It is wrong to try to have a physical relationship with someone's marriage partner. It is wrong to slander or talk bad about someone because you feel jealous or you don't like that person, and so on.

God created us with a will and with the ability and freedom to do the right thing or the wrong thing. We sin when we don't do what is right, when we violate our conscience, when we hurt ourselves or others.

Two Different Kinds of People

There are sincere people that admit that they are not perfect and acknowledge that sometimes they violate their conscience and do wrong things (sin).

As soon as they ask God to help them do the right things, seek to experience God in their lives, and try to understand His word, God will guide these people and will reveal more of Himself and His word to them.

When they talk to God by faith, ask Him to forgive them, and depend on His love, mercy, and grace to cover them, God saves them.

But there are other people who refuse to admit that because they are not perfect, they do many wrong things. They refuse to acknowledge God or seek His help to stop doing what they know is wrong and do what they know is right. They refuse to have faith that God will provide the solution to their wrong attitude and behavior.

Some people, unfortunately, are too prideful to depend on God to save them from the consequences of their sins (have mercy on them). They suppress the Truth that God gave them about Himself and themselves.

For wrong reasons, they refuse to examine the evidence or gain the knowledge that would lead them in the direction of knowing God and His word.

They reject God because they desire to give themselves the freedom to do wrong things, which they know God would not approve (Romans 1:18-21).

You find some of these people spending their time doing trivial things or things which harm them or harm others.

They will not spend time to seek or know God. These people lose now and forever. They fail to realize that the reason God wants to stop them from doing everything they desire is because God does not want them to suffer the horrible consequences of doing wrong. As an example, having sex freely could hurt them physically (with a sexual disease) and will eventually hurt themselves and others emotionally.

RIGHTEOUS THROUGH FAITH

You might consider yourself to be a good person when you compare yourself to others, but no one is good enough to enter heaven. The Bible tells us,

> No one can ever be made right with God by doing what the law commands. The law simply shows us how sinful we are. But now God has shown us a way to be made right with him without keeping the requirements of the law. . . . We are made right with God by placing our faith in Jesus Christ" (Romans 3:20-22).

God's law is a reflection of His perfect standard. Just as we recognize a bent line when we place it next to a straight line; in a similar way, the law shows us how far from perfect we really are.

In the just courtroom of heaven, before God the righteous and just Judge, we stand. We will not be able to plead innocent because we are not innocent of sin. The verdict is *Guilty*. We will suffer as a natural consequence of the wrong we did, but happy is the person who is forgiven.

God inspired the prophet David to write, "Blessed is he whose transgressions are forgiven, whose sins are covered. Blessed is the man whose sin the Lord does not count against him" (Psalm 32:1-2).

Before I received God's forgiveness, I clearly remember struggling as if I were climbing a mountain with a heavy backpack. When I repented and placed my faith in Jesus, I felt so light, so free, so clean, so forgiven. I danced and ran for joy!

Jesus Christ removed the barrier between God and me. Out of His matchless love for me, God placed my debt of sin on Jesus who willingly paid the price.

I would like to share a story with you that clarifies this. Once there was a rich king. He was also the lawgiver and supreme judge of his kingdom. One day, his beloved son committed serious violations of the law. The penalty for those violations amounted to paying a very large fine which his son did not have. The king was a just judge and did not want to violate his own laws, so he ordered his son to pay this fine. The son was terrified because he knew that according to the law of his kingdom, if he did not pay this fine, he would have to go to prison for a long time.

The son realized his mistakes and repented with all his heart for breaking the laws. To save him, his father, the king, decided to pay the fine from his own personal finances. Humbly and joyfully, the son accepted his father's gift. Out of his gratitude and love for his father, the son dedicated the rest of his life to serving his father and his kingdom.

There are similarities between this story and our relationship with God. God personally paid the price that we owed for violating His laws. It is up to us to joyfully accept that payment.

ALL OF US NEED GOD'S GRACE

My friend, none of us can say with a clear conscience, "I have never done anything wrong. I am not a sinner." It takes only one sin to become a sinner. For example, at some time in our lives, all of us have lied, maybe took something that was not ours (stolen), hated somebody, talked bad about others, and so on. Are you willing to admit you have sinned in some way? Will you acknowledge that you are in need of God's mercy and grace? The fantastic news is that Jesus dealt with our problem of sin and provided the solution once and for all.

ILLUSTRATION OF GOD'S GIFT OF GRACE

God wants you to obtain and enjoy His salvation as a gift. If you tried to earn it by your own efforts, you could not do it because you don't deserve it. But if you ask God to save you because of your trust in Jesus. He will do so gladly because He loves you. Grace is undeserved favor. The following story demonstrates God's gift of grace:

A poor and hungry woman, tired from walking, saw a garden full of fruits and tried to buy some, but the gardener refused to take her money. The woman continued to plead with the gardener, but he still refused to sell her the fruit.

The king's son, overheard the woman's pleading and told her, "My father owns this garden and everything you see around it. He's not a merchant and he doesn't need your money. You can't buy his fruit. But if you merely ask for it and believe that he will give it to you as a gift, he will." The woman joyfully accepted the king's gracious gift. The prince picked up an abundance of the most perfect fruit in the garden and gave the woman all she needed.

Likewise, we cannot buy our own salvation. But because of His deep and amazing love toward us, God offers us salvation as a free gift.

> For it is by grace you have been saved, through faith—and this not from yourselves, it is the gift

of God—not by works, so that no one can boast (Ephesians 2:8-9).

Realizing we are desperately in need of God's grace humbles us—receiving God's grace uplifts us.

FORGIVENESS THROUGH FAITH

God will declare *not guilty* (justified) all who believe Jesus died on the cross to pay the penalty for their sins:

> Since we have been made right in God's sight by faith, we have peace with God because of what Jesus Christ, our Lord, has done for us (Romans 5:1).

God is asking you to respond in faith so you can experience His grace and forgiveness to save your soul from suffering forever.

I remember when I was a child in Egypt, I would occasionally get into trouble. My father owned the building where his legal practice was located. On the ground floor was his office and we lived upstairs. Many times I invited my friends to play soccer in the hallway outside his office. It was only a short matter of time before our soccer ball broke a light bulb. Another time, it hit one of my father's clients. Sometimes the ball would hit the glass door of his office.

These disturbances, along with the loud, joyful yelling and screaming, often interrupted his business conversations. Soon afterward, my father would come home with that certain look that told me I'm in trouble. So I would run to my mother crying, hiding behind her big body, trusting that through her I would be safe and forgiven. Although my father was angry, when he saw my mother's beautiful face and my repentant heart, often times he let me go unpunished.

Other times, my strong, big mother would gather me in her arms and shield me. When my father tried to spank me, his newspaper, belt, or hand would fall on her instead of me.

These memories always remind me of the time I ran to Jesus and put my trust in Him. It was then that I truly experienced God's forgiveness. Jesus covered me with His righteousness and shielded me from punishment just as the Bible states:

> It is by the name of Jesus Christ . . . salvation is found in no one else, for there is no other name under heaven given to men by which we must be saved (Acts 4:10-12).

God knocks softly on the door of your heart. If you were to ask me, "Samy, how do you know?" I would answer, that He knocked on the door of my heart years ago and I invited Him in. I have not been the same since.

Jesus said, "Here I am! I stand at the door and knock. If anyone hears My voice and opens the door, I will come in" (Revelation 3:20).

Can you hear Him knocking? He desires to have a personal relationship with you. Will you open the door for Him by faith and allow Him to enter your life and be your Lord and Friend? If your answer is yes, God will greet you face to face and this will be the best decision you'll ever make in your life. God is inviting you to depend on His grace, mercy, and love.

SALVATION IS IMMEDIATE

Even if you feel you're the worst person in the world and don't deserve forgiveness, you really can be forgiven and know today that you will enjoy eternal life with God.

We know this is true because while Jesus hung on the cross, He told a sinful criminal hanging on the cross next to Him, "Today you will be with Me in paradise" (Luke 23:43). God knew this man had a believing and repentant heart; and because of his faith in Jesus, God accepted him into heaven. God did this even though his sins far outweighed his good works.

TRUE CHRISTIANS DON'T WANT TO DO WRONG

Many people claim to be Christians but they live far from God. These people are deceived. No true follower of Christ purposely continues to violate his or her conscience and do wrong things (sin).

Christ gives His true followers the desire and power to do good. We read in the Bible that Jesus "gave his life to free us from every kind of sin, to cleanse us, and to make us his very own people, totally committed to doing good deeds" (Titus 2:14).

SPIRITUAL GROWTH IS A PROCESS

Just as infants grow physically, believers in Christ grow spiritually. As the followers of Christ continue to grow, they stumble and fall short of the perfect standard of their holy God. They struggle against sin and Satan. Gradually they mature in their spiritual lives. When Christians do something wrong (sin), they can take comfort in God's promise to always forgive them when they confess and repent. This glorious promise is found in 1 John 1:9:

> If we confess our sins, He is faithful and just and will forgive us our sins and purify us from all unrighteousness.

Believers in Christ rejoice that God does not leave them to live life alone. The Holy Spirit empowers them to overcome temptations and to improve their character. "For God is working in you giving you the desire and the power to do what pleases him" (Philippians 2:13).

By the way, God will never expect you to do something without giving you the power to do it. The Bible assures us that "God, who began the good work within you, will continue his work until it is finally finished" (Philippians 1:6).

The Bible also tells us that God is constantly working in us, to change us to be the most wonderful people we can possibly be. We read in the Bible:

> The Holy Spirit produces this kind of fruit in our lives: Love, joy, peace, patience, kindness, goodness, faithfulness, gentleness and self control (Galatians 5:22-23).

6

⚬∿⚬

God Is Love

The glorious revelation in the Bible is that God loves each person unconditionally. Every person can know God personally and experience His love, blessings, and salvation.

THE STORY OF THE REBELLIOUS SON

The Bible shows God's astonishing love even for those who are recklessly wasting their lives. In Luke chapter 15, Jesus teaches us through an interesting story. Jesus describes the insulting actions of a younger son who decided to leave his family; but first, he asked his father for his share of the inheritance. It was a selfish and disloyal desire because according to Middle Eastern culture, it is shameful for a son to do that while his father was still alive. A son had the responsibility to help his family until his father died. Then he could receive his inheritance.

But the rebellious son took the money, left his father's house, and went far away to squander the wealth in wild living. But then a famine occurred and he ran out of money. Let's read what happened next:

> When he [the rebellious, prodigal son] came to his senses, he said, "How many of my father's hired men have food to spare and here I am starving to death! I will set out and go back to my father and say to him: 'Father, I have sinned against heaven and against you. I am no longer worthy to be called your son; make me like one of your hired men.'" So he got up and went to his father.

> But while he was still a long way off, his father saw him and was filled with compassion for him; he ran to his son, threw his arms around him and kissed him.

> The son said to him, "Father, I have sinned against heaven and against you. I am no longer worthy to be called your son."

> But the father said to his servants, "Quick! Bring the best robe and put it on him. Put a ring on his finger and sandals on his feet. Bring the fattened calf and kill it. Let's have a feast and celebrate. For this son of mine was dead and is alive again; he was lost and is found." So they began to celebrate.

Meanwhile, the older son was in the field. When he came near the house, he heard music and dancing. So he called one of the servants and asked him what was going on. "Your brother has come," he replied, "and your father has killed the fattened calf because he has him back safe and sound." The older brother became angry and refused to go in. So his father went out and pleaded with him. But he answered his father, "Look! All these years I've been slaving for you and never disobeyed your orders. Yet you never gave me even a young goat so I could celebrate with my friends. But when this son of yours who has squandered your property with prostitutes comes home, you kill the fattened calf for him!"

"My son," the father said, "you are always with me, and everything I have is yours. But we had to celebrate and be glad, because this brother of yours was dead and is alive again; he was lost and is found" (Luke 15:17-32).

INTERPRETATION OF THE STORY

This story could also be called, "The Story of the Loving Father." Even though the disloyal son had brought disgrace to his family, the father was waiting, hoping that his son would come back. During this time apart, he was most likely grieving as he thought about his son living without the love and comfort of his family. He loved him passionately and was hurting deeply because he felt that his son was hurting, too.

As soon as the father saw his son, he spontaneously ran out to welcome him, demonstrating his love. Nothing else mattered to him, for the father had never ceased to love his son. He still loved him even when his son hurt him and squandered his inheritance in wild living.

Even though the prodigal son's wrong actions broke his relationship with his father, the father did not ask him to earn his forgiveness. Jesus is teaching us through this story that God's love for each one of us is never rooted in our worthiness, but rather, in His own nature. Jesus is teaching that God's love is undeserved. God loves the people who are far from Him and eagerly awaits their return because He knows that they are not happy when they are far from Him. The heavenly Father patiently waits for the return of even the worst person because He loves all people and desires to give everyone the most wonderful life.

God wants to guide every person to Himself and to salvation. "This is good, and pleases God our Savior, who wants everyone to be saved and to understand the truth" (1 Timothy 2:3-4).

YOU ARE INVITED TO BECOME GOD'S CHILD

God allows us to enter into a wonderful relationship with Him so that we can be His children: "Yet to all who received Him [Jesus], to those who believed in His name, He gave the right to become children of God—children born not of natural descent, nor from human decision or a husband's will, but born of God" (John 1:12-13). The moment you believe in Jesus, a miracle takes place—you are born of God's Spirit and become a child of God.

This new relationship between God and you leads to an interactive and personal love. Even though God loves everybody, the moment you are born of His Spirit, God feels the most irresistible attachment to you.

I remember seeing a father holding a newborn baby in his hands. To him and his wife, this was the most precious baby in the world. "Isn't the baby gorgeous?" he asked me? I was too distracted by the crying, spitting, and smell to answer. Obviously, the parents appreciated the beauty of their baby much more than I did.

Through demonstration of the parents' love for their newborn baby, God showed me that He loves me, in spite of my imperfections, much more than these parents could ever love their baby. I could feel God saying to me, "Even though I love every living person, Samy, you are My child. You are more special to Me than the people that haven't yet become My children. I know all your mistakes, past failures, and present weaknesses. Regardless of everything wrong you might have done, you are My most treasured and precious possession. You are born of My Spirit and you are My child! You are a part of Me and I am part of you."

Ever since I became a child of God in February 1976, I have been enjoying God's perfect, fatherhood heart.

GOD DESIRES TO BE YOUR PERFECT FATHER

All that a perfect father wants to be to his children, God is and will be to you when you are born of His Spirit and approach Him in prayer. Because you are His child, there is nothing that can separate you from His love (Romans 8:38-39). God feels the most irresistible attraction toward all His children.

We read in the Bible, "See how very much our Father loves us, for he calls us his children, and that is what we are!" (1 John 3:1).

"Father" is the Christian name for God; so when Jesus instructed His disciples how to pray, He said to address God as "our Father" (Matthew 6). He also said to His disciples, "The Father Himself loves you" (John 16:27).

My precious reader, only through knowing God as your Father can you enjoy the fullness of His deep love for you, be assured of His goodwill, and start experiencing His wonderful plans for your life.

God raises us to the highest level because He has made us His children. We still bow down before Him and approach His throne with awe; and at the same time, we have peace and confidence because we know that He is our gracious heavenly Father.

This is one of the most amazing manifestations of the love of God. We were orphans bound as slaves in Satan's kingdom—robbed of dignity, peace, and joy of family. We were filthy, poor, and helpless, destined to spend eternity separated from God. We were suffering because of our sin and miserable condition.

It is truly amazing that the Bible revealed God as the most noble and powerful King who fought Satan on our behalf and won the battle through Jesus Christ's death and resurrection. You will discover throughout this book how Jesus broke the chains that were binding us and destroyed the walls separating us from God and from freedom.

Now God is personally inviting you; he is in essence saying, "I want to cleanse you and forgive you. I want you to come to Me. I want you to be part of My kingdom. I want to adopt you into My royal family. You will bear My name and share My kingdom. You will live with Me forever."

The Bible clearly assures us, "Now if we are children, then we are heirs" (Romans 8:17). We will always be God's children. While a servant must work to earn his place in his master's house, we as God's children cannot be dismissed. We are not frightened of God as a Master whose acceptance we have to strive to obtain.

It is so comforting to know that Jesus said, "Don't be afraid . . . for it gives your Father great happiness to give you the kingdom" (Luke 12:32). Heaven will be our home because God has made us His children.

I remember when my Father tried to persuade me to stay in Egypt; he told me, "Why do you want to go to

America? My son, everything I have, (my legal firm, my property), one day will be yours to enjoy."

Because God is our Father, we can rejoice in knowing that one day we will share His kingdom and enjoy His glorious presence forever. However, when we insist on doing something wrong, God does chasten His children here on earth for the purpose of correcting them (Hebrews 12:5-11). But we also have assurance that His discipline is accompanied by unconditional love and forgiveness.

My precious friend, God wants you to become a citizen in His heavenly kingdom. God is the King and He desires to make you His royal child.

WHO IS THIS GOD THAT RULES THE UNIVERSE?

In the Gospel, the most prevalent characteristic revealed about God is that "God is love" (1 John 4:8). God loves us because of who He is and He offers to care for us now and forever.

God's heart overflows with love for you and me. We read in the Bible, "But God demonstrates His own love for us in this: while we were still sinners, Christ died for us" (Romans 5:8). God did the greatest thing He could possibly do to reveal His deep, strong, and perfect love for you and me. No better proof can be given to mankind than this.

EXPERIENCE GOD'S LOVE THROUGH THE HOLY SPIRIT

God gives us the Holy Spirit to dwell within us and make us conscious of His love toward us. The Holy Spirit takes up residence in us the moment we place our faith in Christ as our Savior, which enables us to experience God's fatherly love in our hearts and souls. The Bible promises, "And this hope will not lead to disappointment for we know how dearly God loves us, because he has given us the Holy Spirit to fill our hearts with his love" (Romans 5:5).

We also read, "And because we are his children, God has sent the Spirit of his son into our hearts, prompting us to call out, 'Abba Father.' Now you are no longer a slave but God's own child. And since you are his child, God has made you his heir" (Galatians 4:6-7).

The love of the heavenly Father, made manifest in Jesus Christ, becomes a reality in our hearts and lives through the Holy Spirit whom God placed within our hearts. We read in the Bible, "You have not received a spirit that makes you fearful slaves. Instead, you received God's Spirit when he adopted you as his own children. Now we call him 'Abba, Father.' for his Spirit joins with our Spirit to affirm that we are God's children" (Romans 8:15-16).

To make this fact clearer to you, I will share with you a story of a man who adopted a child. After all the forms have been filled out, the papers processed, and the adoption became legal, the moment comes when this kind man takes the child to his home. The child is shown a room filled with toys. The man gently says to the child, "Do you see this beautiful room? This is your room. Do you see all of these toys? These are your toys. This house is your house, and I am your father who loves you." Then he gives the child a big, warm hug. Imagine how valuable and glorious this child must have felt in these precious moments. You, too, will have the most awesome experience when the Holy Spirit enters your life.

The Holy Spirit is the deposit guaranteeing your inheritance until you acquire possession of it. The seal of God will be upon you. The Holy Spirit will give you the assurance that your adoption as God's child is forever.

A WORD FROM MY HEART

Beloved reader, I remember clearly the time I put my faith in Jesus (February 17, 1976). I felt God embracing me. And now, after thirty-five years, I can easily say that I am in love with God. He is worthy of my life and my affection. I love Him with all my heart. I want to know Him more deeply, to serve Him more, and to praise Him. My pleasure and satisfaction are found in giving Him every day of my life.

I can say as the apostle Paul did, "For Christ's love controls us" (2 Corinthians 5:14). I mean, God's love compels me to forget myself and joyfully submit my life into God's hand. I become His, not out of fear, obligation, or out of what I could get from Him, but just because I love Him.

Similarly, when I was a child, I used to ask my parents to buy me things. But after growing up and appreciating their love for me, I became more interested in spending time with them and doing things for them.

My purpose for writing this book is to help you experience in your own heart God's deep and personal love for you. My friend, you, too, can experience God as your loving, heavenly Father. You can feel His embrace in your heart and enjoy His very presence within you when you step out in faith and tell God that you don't want to continue living far from Him anymore and that you are sorry you did not always do what was right. You made mistakes (you sinned) and now you believe that Jesus Christ died to pay the penalty for everything you've done wrong.

God will enter your life. You will experience His forgiveness, wonderful peace, and love immediately right where you are, and you will be a very happy person because of it.

You will feel the heavenly Father's loving arms drawing you to His bosom. Then you will find yourself drawn to Him with the most irresistible attraction. You will start falling in love with Him from the depth of your being! I cannot begin to describe to you how wonderful you will feel when you realize that you have become a child to the creator of the universe.

As you walk with God by faith, grow in your relationship with Him, learn more about Him, and experience more of Him, satisfaction and contentment will be the hallmark of your life. You will be a different person.

7

∽

God's Love
Manifested through the Story of Adam

The desire of God's heart—to fellowship with man and to relate to you personally—is revealed through His first creation, Adam.

ADAM CREATED PERFECT BY GOD

According to the Bible, God created people so that He would enjoy beautiful fellowship with them. To accomplish this, God created Adam and Eve in perfect condition and placed them in the Garden of Eden where he had a personal relationship with them. God loved them and gave them a beautiful place to live with an awesome view—the perfect circumstances to enjoy life forever.

In the garden, God gave them permission to eat from all the trees except one.

Having experienced God's love, they should have known and trusted that God's instruction was good and in their best interests. They should have expressed their gratitude and love for God by obeying His word.

ADAM'S DISOBEDIENCE SEPARATED HIM FROM GOD

God's intention for his creation to live a perfect, sinless life was fulfilled while Adam walked in fellowship with Him. But Adam disobeyed God; and as a result, his relationship with God was broken. The prophet Isaiah declared, "Your iniquities have separated you from your God" (Isaiah 59:1-2).

Adam's iniquity (sin) caused separation between mankind and the holy God. Why? Because the moment Adam and Eve chose to eat the fruit from the forbidden tree, they intentionally violated the authority of God. Although Adam was created morally pure—in the image of God—he lost the ability to be completely moral when he disobeyed his Creator.

SIN INFECTED ALL HUMANITY

Since Adam was the first human, we can call him the father of all humankind. We all originate from him. Therefore, his disobedience affected all the members of his family and God's image in mankind became distorted.

One of my friends said to me, "It's not fair that we all have to suffer because Adam and Eve disobeyed God that one time."

I explained to him that this principle is logical and can be seen even today. For example, when a nation's leader wages war, people are killed and a whole country can suffer from this one leader's wrong decision. Another example is when parents live an immoral lifestyle—lying, cheating, stealing, committing adultery. Their children often suffer emotionally, socially, and sometimes physically as a result of their parents' disobedience to God's will.

Sin (disobeying God) is a contagious disease that started in Adam and has since spread like an epidemic throughout all of mankind. Fallen humanity experiences the effects of this epidemic daily through self-centeredness (selfishness), jealousy, envy, hatred, etc.

Surely we can testify that we have indulged in wrongdoing. Many times we have violated our conscience and yielded to our selfish nature, disregarding the rights and interests of others. We have done this because even within the best of all human hearts remains an evil nature.

THE DEVASTATING CONSEQUENCES OF SIN

God created Adam and Eve as perfect, sinless human beings who would live happily forever, and He forewarned Adam of the devastating consequences of disobedience: "If you eat its fruit, you are sure to die" (Genesis 2:17).

Adam did eat the forbidden fruit; and at that moment, the Bible states that death entered the world: "Adam's sin brought death, so death spread to everyone, for everyone sinned" (Romans 5:12). Sin sentences us to a slow death. It cuts us off from God's presence, like a flower plucked from its source of life. It is just a matter of time before that flower dies completely.

As a natural consequence of sin, our body, spirit, and soul are now and eternally separated from God, our source of life. No amount of good works or efforts on our part can bridge the distance between us and God. All people continue to fall short of the perfect life God created us to live because sin is now an integral part of human nature.

THE SOLUTION

To restore our relationship with God, Christ voluntarily paid the price for all the wrong we have committed and ever will commit. The apostle Paul said, "[Jesus] loved me and gave Himself for me" (Galatians 2:20).

God's judgment against sin fell upon Jesus. In Jesus, we see an accurate picture of the balance between God's righteous anger and God's love—love in its purest and deepest sense.

Jesus Is Your Ticket to Heaven

We read in the Bible, "So you see, just as death came into the world through a man, now the resurrection from the dead has begun through another man. Just as everyone dies because we all belong to Adam, everyone who belongs to Christ will be given new life" (1 Corinthians 15:21-22).

As a light bulb becomes full of light when connected with electrical power, your life will come alive when you put your faith in Jesus Christ as your Savior. You will be united to God and start fulfilling the purpose for which you were created.

Jesus taught, "I tell you the truth, no one can see the kingdom of God unless he is born-again" (John 3:3).

To be born-again means to be transformed in the very depths of your being. At that time, the Holy Spirit (God) comes to dwell within you and gives you many spiritual blessings—a new heart with new affections and desires, new power, and a new destination. You develop a new view of life and of people around you (God's perspective), a new nature, and a new purpose! The Bible declares, "This means that anyone who belongs to Christ has become a new person. The old life is gone, a new life has begun" (2 Corinthians 5:17).

This new birth happens as a result of repentance. According to the Bible, repentance is making a decision and commitment to stop doing wrong things (forsake all sins). Repentance involves humbling yourself and receiving God's mercy and grace through faith in Jesus.

The wonderful truth is that as soon as you do that and believe in what Jesus Christ has done for you on the cross, you will be born again. Upon your new birth, you will begin to enjoy a personal and loving relationship with your Creator. You will be in the right position to receive the abundant life and blessings God is longing to give you. You will be like a child in the house of his loving father.

My dear reader, will you decide to take a step of faith? Will you demonstrate your faith through a simple and yet most vital decision? Will you declare with your mouth to God that you believe and rely on Jesus' death on the cross to pay the penalty for your sins?

The decision is as simple as trusting a chair to hold your weight when you sit on it. When you put your faith in Jesus for the forgiveness of anything wrong you did— not in yourself or your works or anything else—you will experience God's forgiveness and enjoy amazing rest.

THE HOLY SPIRIT DWELLS WITHIN THE TRUE FOLLOWERS OF CHRIST

True believers and followers of Christ are people who have experienced a new birth. Many people claim to be Christians; perhaps they have Christian parents, received

Christian education, or they accept that Christianity is a good religion to be a part of. They might attend a church, try to do good works, or agree with Christian beliefs intellectually. They might even be serving in a church. However, none of those things can make someone a child of God.

Only those people who experience the new birth become part of God's family. The evidence of this new birth is the presence of the Holy Spirit within, confirming that they are God's children.

You Will Have the Best Life

The Holy Spirit within you will help you to realize that God knows you personally and you are special to Him. Through the Holy Spirit, you will be able to hear God speaking to you. God wants you to be in harmony with His instructions so you will not hinder Him from giving you the best life you can ever have.

Jesus Reconciles Us to God Forever

Remember, eternal life was God's original intent for Adam and his descendants; but because of Adam's sin, we forfeited enjoying God's presence and kingdom forever. But God provided a way for us to re-establish an eternal relationship with Him—He sent us Jesus. What awesome glad news! Jesus reconciles us to God forever!

The Bible tells us:

And all of this is a gift from God, who brought us back to himself through Christ. . . . For God was in Christ, reconciling the world to himself, no longer counting people's sins against them (2 Corinthians 5:18-19).

Someone said to me, "It doesn't seem fair that Jesus paid the price for my sins. Everyone must make amends for their own wrong choices."

My answer to him was that this incredible sacrifice is not something we requested or forced God to do. God did this for us—as a gift. And God is simply asking us to accept His gift.

I also reminded my friend that Jesus freely chose to rescue us when He said, "I sacrifice my life. . . . No one can take my life from me. I sacrifice it voluntarily" (John 10:17-18).

A few times, I have seen fathers and mothers sacrifice their lives in order to save their children's lives. Some people even sacrifice their lives for their country. Similarly, Jesus said that "He did not come to be served, but to serve, and to give His life as a ransom for many" (Matthew 20:28).

Please allow me to illustrate this ultimate act of love through another story: One day, a young man committed murder. The police chased after him on the ground and in the air, but he managed to get home to his family. His father was shocked to see that his son's clothing was stained with blood. The son confessed to his father that he had just killed someone and that the police sirens they were hearing and the helicopter overhead was after him.

The father quickly told his son to take off his clothes. As the police pounded on the door, the father put on his son's clothing and the son put on his father's. The police barged in and when they saw the father's clothes stained with blood, they arrested him. The father paid for his son's crime. This reminds me of the love that Jesus described:

> Greater love has no one than this, than to lay down his life for his friends (John 15:13).

Imagine a door that opens into heaven and gives you access to the presence of God. There is such a door. Jesus said, "I am the gate; whoever enters through Me will be saved" (John 10:9).

It is Jesus' mission to make it possible for us to have fellowship with God: "Christ suffered for our sins once for all time . . . to bring you safely home to God" (1 Peter 3:18).

A WORD FROM MY HEART

Beloved reader, are you burdened or worried? Do you feel alone? Do you feel emotionally and spiritually thirsty? God does not desire for you to live life this way.

Jesus promised, "If anyone is thirsty, let him come to Me and drink" (John 7:37). As water satisfies your body, Jesus promises He will satisfy your heart.

Your soul may be thirsty, seeking to find happiness everywhere, without success. When you come to Jesus and believe in Him and follow His teachings, you will be satisfied now and forever.

8

God's Love Manifested through the Story of Abraham

In the Bible, Abraham is described as the friend of God (James 2:23). This implies that God shared with Abraham many of His secret plans for the future, which you are about to learn as well.

THE DIFFICULT TEST OF ABRAHAM'S FAITH

God said to Abraham:

> Take your son, your only son, Isaac, whom you love, and go to the region of Moriah. Sacrifice him there as a burnt offering on one of the mountains I will tell you about (Genesis 22:1-2).

Abraham must have thought deeply about God's shocking and apparently immoral command. For God had promised Abraham that through his son, Isaac, he would have many descendants: "as numerous as the stars in the sky and as countless as the sand on the seashore" (Genesis 15:5 and 32:12).

ABRAHAM TRUSTED GOD

Abraham no doubt wondered, "If I sacrifice my son, Isaac, as God commanded of me, how will I be able to have many descendants, as God promised to me?" But Abraham believed in God's promises, His faithfulness, and His righteousness. He concluded that the only way Isaac could beget offspring—after being sacrificed—would be for God to raise him from the dead.

Abraham reasoned that since God gave him a son when it was naturally impossible to have one (he and Sarah were too old to have children when Isaac was born), then God could also bring that son back to life. For that reason, Abraham knew that sacrificing his son was not the same as idolaters sacrificing their children to false gods, which was common practice in his time. So Abraham prepared to sacrifice his son, trusting completely in the holy character of God.

ABRAHAM PASSED THE TEST

The Bible makes it clear that Abraham passed this great test of faith:

> It was by faith that Abraham offered Isaac as a sacrifice when God was testing him. Abraham, who had received God's promises, was ready to

sacrifice his only son, Isaac, even though God had told him, "Isaac is the son through whom your descendents will be counted." Abraham reasoned that if Isaac died, God was able to bring him back to life again. And in a sense, Abraham did receive his son back from the dead (Hebrews 11:17-19).

ABRAHAM'S PROFOUND FAITH

Abraham's decision to obey God and sacrifice his son was not simply mindless, blind, uncomprehending submission to the will of God. Abraham believed that God would always be faithful to His word. He realized that somehow God would make good on His promise and give him many descendants through Isaac in spite of sacrificing him.

GOD'S COVENANT WITH ABRAHAM

We see the prominence of Abraham in the Bible. God promised him, "Through your offspring all nations [families] on earth will be blessed" (Genesis 12:3).

God told Abraham, "As for Me, this is My covenant with you: You will be the father of many nations" (Genesis 17:4). Abraham considered why he was made a blessing for mankind and the father of a multitude of people. Abraham realized that he resembled the heavenly Father as a human prototype of God Himself.

Abraham surely also realized that Isaac's miraculous birth, upcoming sacrifice, resurrection from the dead, and the innumerable descendants promised to him were foreshadowing a reality yet to come.

ABRAHAM FORESAW THE GOOD NEWS OF A GREATER SACRIFICE

Jesus told the Jews that Abraham foresaw the heart of the gospel: "Your father Abraham rejoiced at the thought of seeing My day; he saw it and was glad" (John 8:56).

God revealed to His friend, Abraham, His plan of salvation and the coming blessing to mankind. He understood that the heavenly Father would have a Son born miraculously into this world. The Son would be offered as a sacrifice by the hand of His own Father. The Son would rise from the dead and be the source of blessings to the world.

A PROPHETIC CONVERSATION BETWEEN ABRAHAM AND ISAAC

When they reached the place for the sacrifice, Isaac asked his father, Abraham, "The fire and wood are here, but where is the lamb for the burnt offering?" Abraham did not know God would provide a substitute in place of Isaac. He truly believed he would have to sacrifice his son, so Abraham replied to Isaac, "God Himself will provide the lamb for the burnt offering, my son" (Genesis 22:7-8).

The original words of this verse in Hebrew say in effect, "God will give the Lamb from His very own being."

Through this experience, God revealed to His friend, Abraham, that someday He would send His own Son to die for the sins of the world and that any person who trusts in God's saving grace will be blessed and saved. Beloved reader, God has actually given you Himself—the ultimate gift.

This reminds me of a wealthy couple who sat down with a marriage counselor to solve their marital problems. Angrily, the husband said, "I don't understand my wife's problem. I gave her a diamond ring for our wedding anniversary. I bought a house in her name, and I gave her money to spend on herself every month."

After he listed everything he gave her, the wife replied, "Yes, it is true, Jack. You have given me everything." With tears running from her eyes, she continued, "Everything except yourself!"

How awesome it is to realize that 2,000 years after God asked Abraham to sacrifice his son, Isaac, on Mount Moriah, Jesus was crucified on that same mount. In this way, Genesis chapter 22 is a foreshadowing of the crucifixion of Jesus Christ, which occurred according to God's plan of salvation for mankind. It is amazing and significant to find the Christian message, indeed the heart of the gospel, written all over the Jewish holy Scriptures.

ABRAHAM'S RIGHTEOUSNESS

In spite of Abraham's sins, which are recorded in the Bible, God forgave Abraham and declared him to be righteous. Abraham's faith in God and in His ability to perform what He had promised was accepted by God as righteousness. "Abram [Abraham] believed the Lord, and the Lord counted him as righteous because of his faith" (Genesis 15:6).

Abraham's faith was an awesome example because he didn't simply or merely bow to God's command, he believed that God's command was consistent with God's faithfulness. Abraham depended on the righteousness, goodness, and trustworthiness of God. Thus his faith gave glory to God. This "faith" principle is explained in the Bible:

> Abraham never wavered in believing God's promise. In fact, his faith grew stronger, and in this he brought glory to God.

> He was fully convinced that God is able to do whatever he promises and because of Abraham's faith, God counted him as righteous.

> And when God counted him as righteous, it wasn't just for Abraham's benefit. It was recorded for our benefit, too, assuring us that God will also count us as righteous if we believe in him, the one who raised Jesus our Lord from the dead.

He was handed over to die because of our sins, and he was raised to life to make us right with God (Romans 4:20-25).

GOD'S SACRIFICIAL LOVE FOR US

Have you ever wondered why God asked father Abraham to sacrifice (to give God) his son? It is because a man's own son is more precious to his heart than anything else. If Abraham was willing to give up his own son for God, then he was prepared to give God anything and everything. Therefore, the best way for God to test Abraham's love for Him was to command him to sacrifice his son.

Abraham had to make a choice between his love for God and his love for his son. Abraham's willingness to sacrifice his son for God proved that he loved God more than he loved his son or anything else in life.

When God commanded Abraham to sacrifice his son, Isaac, Abraham no doubt suffered deeply as a father. He was ripped at the depth of his being as he led his living son to sacrifice him by his own hand. By following God's command, Abraham proved that he had perfect, sacrificial love for God.

My dear reader, do you think God would require a deeper demonstration of love from us than He would demonstrate to us?

The significant question here is this: can a man's love for God (such as Abraham's) surpass God's love for mankind? The logical answer is that God never asked any man, including Abraham, to do more for Him than He was willing to do for us.

God bestowed on us the greatest form of love by giving His own Son, whose presence He enjoyed from all eternity. God sacrificed what was most precious to His heart. The Bible shows us that God's love for Abraham and for us, in Christ, far surpassed Abraham's love for God.

This truth is exactly what God wants you to discover, my dear friend. God expressed His perfect love for you:

> He who did not spare His own Son, but gave Him up for us all—how will He not also, along with Him, graciously give us all things? (Romans 8:32).

Here we see God's heart aflame with love for mankind.

LEADING WITH SACRIFICIAL LOVE

Leaders come in many forms. The battles of World War II gives us a chance to examine a couple of them. For example, one military commander leading a British unit ordered his troops to advance into the battlefield. On hearing the news that 3,250 of his troops were killed and 750 wounded, he replied, "Is that all? I thought there'd be more," and continued drinking his coffee with a cold heart.

James, another military commander leading a different British unit, saw his soldiers surrounded by the enemy. He ordered them to engage in warfare and joined them on the front lines. Against all odds, he was able to lead them to victory. He saved the lives of most of his soldiers, although he was chopped to pieces. He laid down his life for his men.

The second leader shows us a glimpse of how God has led His people to victory, giving of Himself for our sake. God's love is perfect.

The true test and measure of love is sacrifice. When you look at the cross and at Jesus who hung upon it, you see the depth and intensity of God's infinite and eternal love for you.

> But God demonstrates His own love for us in this: While we were still sinners, Christ died for us (Romans 5:8).

Jesus is God's most precious gift to you. Will you receive His gift by opening your heart to Jesus right now?

GOD PROVIDED A SUBSTITUTE SACRIFICE

Going back to the story of Abraham, he was about to sacrifice his son, Isaac, but God set his son free. Did God then simply allow the prophet Abraham to take his son and go home? No. God chose only one way to free Abraham's son—by providing a ram to be offered in place of Isaac (Genesis 22:13).

Likewise, my friend, it is God who rescued each one of us from death by offering a sacrifice that He alone provided. John the Baptist knew that Jesus was this sacrifice. When he saw Jesus coming toward him, he proclaimed, "Look! The Lamb of God, who takes away the sin of the world!" (John 1:29).

Even the prophet Isaiah, inspired of God, prophesied about the coming of Jesus (Messiah) and recognized Him to be this sacrificial Lamb: "He was oppressed and afflicted, yet He did not open His mouth; He was led like a lamb to the slaughter, and as a sheep before its shearers is silent, so He did not open His mouth" (Isaiah 53:7).

The driving force behind God's ultimate sacrifice is His infinite love for us.

THE SACRIFICED RAM REPRESENTED A MUCH GREATER TRUTH

It is true that the ram God provided for Abraham was not guilty; but the shedding of its blood shows how serious sin is. In that way, it was a symbol of the greater sacrifice to come—Jesus Christ, who also was not guilty.

It is clearly stated in the Bible, "For you know that it was not with perishable things . . . that you were redeemed from the empty way of life handed down to you from your forefathers, but with the precious blood of Christ, a lamb without blemish or defect" (1 Peter 1:18-19).

Jesus said, "For this is my blood, which confirms the covenant between God and his people. It is poured out as a sacrifice to forgive the sins of many" (Matthew 26:28). Jesus' death inaugurated the new relationship (covenant or testament) between God and His people.

SHAMUEL AND HIS TRAITOR

When I think about sacrificial love, I am reminded of a story about Shamuel, a noble prince who was trying to protect his people and land from being invaded by an evil, neighboring kingdom.

One night, he planned a surprise attack. But the enemy knew that the prince's army was coming. They were waiting for him because somebody had revealed his secret, military plans. Many of his soldiers lost their lives; and ultimately, he lost the battle. Shamuel announced that the traitor would be punished—whipped with one hundred lashes.

In great secrecy, Shamuel's army launched another attack; but again, his enemy knew about it and waited to ambush his soldiers. The prince lost another battle, but this time he discovered the traitor. It was Shamuel's own mother! She was having a romantic relationship with one of the enemy's soldiers.

What a dilemma! What should Shamuel have done? If he exempted his mother from punishment, his followers would correctly say that he is unjust and does not care about his people. The alternative would be even more difficult for Shamuel. Because he loved his mother, how could he mandate a just sentence that would result in the suffering and most likely the death of his beloved mother?

Shamuel addressed his people, "We have lost many battles because of treason. Many of our men have been killed. The law has been broken and punishment shall be executed—one hundred lashes! Justice must be maintained."

The prince's mother was filled with great fear as she was led away to the circle where she would receive her punishment. The executioner lifted his whip. But before the first blow was delivered, Shamuel shouted out, "Wait! Wait! I will take the punishment instead of her." He removed his royal clothes and commanded, "Executioner, you dare not strike me with less force than you would have used on the traitor. I am the person who will take her punishment. Do your duty—strike on!"

Lash after lash struck the back of Shamuel until he collapsed to the ground unconscious. He did, however, survive the lashings contrary to all expectations. Prince Shamuel paid in full the penalty for his beloved mother's offense in order to set her free.

Jesus came to pay a debt He did not owe because we owed a debt we could not pay. God's Word says that, "He personally carried our sins in his body on the cross" (1 Peter 2:24). Jesus taught,

> Greater love has no one than this, that He lay down His life for His friends (John 15:13).

My dear reader, if you were to ask God, "How much do You love me?" He would point to Jesus who hung on the cross and with outstretched arms say, "I love you this much and more."

Biblical scholar, John Stott, expressed the heart of the gospel by saying, "Divine love triumphed over divine wrath by divine self-sacrifice."

9

∾

God Sent Jesus, the Messiah

The Old Testament contains many inspired prophecies of one glorious Savior who one day would be sent by God and be called the "Anointed One" or "Messiah." (Daniel 9:25). These prophecies were written between 400 and 1,500 years before Christ came to earth and contains two different descriptions of the coming Messiah—the first describes Him as the suffering Savior (Isaiah 53) and the second foretells His glory (Daniel 7).

In total, there are sixty-one major prophecies about the Messiah in the Old Testament, and all of them were fulfilled in Jesus! Many books have been written on this subject, such as an outstanding reference material entitled *All the Messianic Prophecies of the Bible* by Herbert Lockyer.[1]

While the Old Testament was written in Hebrew, the New Testament was written in the Greek language. The Greek word for the Messiah is *Ho Christos*, from which comes the English word "Christ." Therefore, Christ means "the Messiah."

The fulfilled prophecies regarding Jesus Christ could not have been fabricated—they were totally beyond human control. Consider the following examples:

- *Place of birth*—The prophet Micah foretold in 700 BC (before the birth of Christ) that the Messiah would be born in Bethlehem (Micah 5:2). The historical fulfillment of this prophecy is found in Matthew 2:1-6 and John 7:42.

- *Virgin birth*—Seven centuries earlier Isaiah prophesied, "Therefore the Lord Himself will give you a sign: The virgin will be with child and will give birth to a Son, and will call Him Immanuel" (Isaiah 7:14). We see the historical fulfillment of this prophecy in the New Testament: "All this took place to fulfill what the Lord had said through the prophet: The virgin will be with child and will give birth to a son, and they will call Him Immanuel which means God with us" (Matthew 1:22-23).

- *Death by crucifixion*—A thousand years before the coming of Christ, the prophet David predicted his crucifixion: "A band of evil men has encircled me, they have pierced my hands and my feet" (Psalm 22:16). The piercing of Jesus is also prophesied in Zechariah 12:10 and later fulfilled as described in John 19:34.

- *Christ's mission*—The prophet Isaiah wrote around 700 BC that "He was pierced for our transgressions, He was crushed for our iniquities; the punishment that brought us peace was upon Him, and by His wounds we are healed. We all, like sheep, have gone astray, each of us has turned to his own way; and the LORD has laid on Him the iniquities of us all" (Isaiah 53:5-6).

THE MESSIAH IS DIVINE

The Bible clearly declares that the predicted Messiah is a divine person. In one of the prophecies, the coming Messiah is given divine names: "For a Child is born to us, a Son is given to us. The government will rest on His shoulders. And he will be called Wonderful Counselor, Mighty God, Everlasting Father, Prince of Peace" (Isaiah 9:6).

The phrase "Everlasting Father" means that this child to be born is eternal and will have the heart of the perfect Father toward His people.

The prophet Isaiah foretold that the coming Messiah would be called Immanuel, which is a Hebrew name meaning "God with us." As written in Isaiah 7:14, "The Lord Himself will give you a sign: The virgin will be with child and will give birth to a son, and will call Him Immanuel." The fulfillment of this prophecy is recorded in Matthew 1:21-23.

Jesus, Son of God and Son of Man

Jesus called Himself "the Son of God." He said, "My Father has entrusted everything to me. No one truly knows the Son except the Father, and no one truly knows the Father except the Son" (Matthew 11:27).

Jesus also called Himself "the Son of Man." He used these titles to make evident His humanity as well as His deity. The prophet Daniel prophesied that the coming Messiah would be divine:

> In my vision at night I looked, and there before me was one like a Son of man, coming with the clouds of heaven. He approached the Ancient of Days and was led into His presence. He was given authority, glory and sovereign power; all peoples, nations and men of every language worshiped Him. His dominion is an everlasting dominion that will not pass away, and His kingdom is one that will never be destroyed (Daniel 7:13-14).

Daniel saw a person like a Son of Man, referring to the fact that He was human in His appearance. He also saw that this person was given sovereign power and would be worshiped by all. Obviously, this One who is like a Son of Man was more than just a man. Clearly the prophets declared in the Holy Scriptures that the coming Messiah would be far superior than a mere prophet.

This verse is one of many biblical references that predicted the coming of the great King who would rescue God's people and establish His eternal kingdom. This expected King came to be called the Messiah. Both the Old and New Testament teach the divine-human nature of the Messiah.

JESUS SAID THAT HE IS THE MESSIAH

The gospel records a conversation between Jesus and a woman who said to Jesus,

> "I know the Messiah is coming—the one who is called Christ. When He comes, He will explain everything to us." Then Jesus told her, "I am the Messiah" (John 4:25-26).

Jews gathered around Jesus and said, "How long will You keep us in suspense? If You are the Christ, tell us plainly." Jesus answered, "I did tell you, but you do not believe. The miracles I do in My Father's name speak for Me" (John 10:24-25).

ANNOUNCEMENT OF THE GOOD NEWS

The prophets of the Old Testament looked forward to the appearance of the glorious Messiah. What a great moment in the history of humanity. The Savior of all people had finally arrived and the good news is announced!

An angel appeared to a group of shepherds in the fields of Bethlehem, and the glory of the Lord shone around them. The angel made this wonderful proclamation:

> I bring you good news that will bring great joy to all people. The savior—yes, The Messiah, the Lord has been born today in Bethlehem (Luke 2:10-11).

OPPOSITION TO THE GOOD NEWS

Many people in the world have never heard or understood why God declared the birth of Jesus Christ to be good news. Of course the enemy, Satan, does not want anyone to know about God's passionate love for humanity.

> Satan is working hard to prevent people from understanding Jesus' nature and mission as revealed throughout the Bible. The Jewish religious teachers asked Jesus' disciples, "Why does your teacher eat with sinners?" Jesus Himself replied,
>
> It is not the healthy who need a doctor, but the sick. I have not come to call the righteous, but sinners to repentance (Mark 2:17).

Jesus came for sinners like you and me.

Jesus' Miracles Attest to his Being the Messiah

During His mission on earth, Christ Jesus displayed great power and authority as no one has ever done. The miracles He performed were definite signs that confirmed He was truly the Savior sent by God.

The Bible prophesied that the coming Messiah would perform specific miracles (Isaiah 35:5-6). Hundreds of years later, when Jesus came to earth, He gave sight to the blind. He gave the lame the ability to walk. He opened deaf ears and did many other wondrous things. Thus, by His miracles, Jesus established that He is the promised Messiah, the Savior of the world.

10

Jesus Is Unique

As you continue reading, you will enjoy discovering the uniqueness of Jesus.

THE VIRGIN BIRTH OF JESUS

> This is how Jesus the Messiah was born. His mother, Mary, was engaged to be married to Joseph. But before the marriage took place, while she was still a virgin, she became pregnant through the power of the Holy Spirit (Matthew 1:18).

> Jesus is the only man in all creation who was born in this unique, divine way.

THE REASON FOR THE VIRGIN BIRTH

The Bible teaches that Jesus is the Son of God who existed throughout all eternity. Therefore, if the eternal

Son of God came to earth in the likeness of a man, He could not have been born as a result of a physical relationship between a man and a woman. Because Jesus is the Son of God, it was absolutely necessary that Jesus be born of a virgin by the power of God's Spirit.

Human life is typically passed on by the male seed. The only exception to this procreation process is Jesus' birth. Jesus was conceived by the Spirit of God. When He came into this world, it was an entry—not a creation.

Since Jesus is not related to a human father, because he came from God, then he could not have been called anything but the Son of God. Jesus' spiritual sonship to the Father explains the necessity and reason for the virgin birth.

Jesus' Virgin Birth Was Prophesied

Jesus was born of a virgin as prophesied by the prophet Isaiah seven centuries before his birth (Isaiah 7:14).

The fact that Jesus had this unique beginning to His life on earth proves that He is unique. The virgin birth supports Jesus' divinity. When the angel Gabriel came to Mary to explain Jesus' miraculous conception, he said, "He will be great and will be called the Son of the Most High. The Holy Spirit will come upon you, and the power of the Most High will overshadow you. So the holy one to be born will be called the Son of God" (Luke 1:32, 35).

THE SINLESSNESS OF JESUS CHRIST

Jesus is the only person who lived throughout His life without committing one single sin. No man or prophet has ever dared to claim himself infallible, but Jesus Christ had complete confidence in His perfection and purity. Therefore, He could boldly ask, "Which of you can truthfully accuse me of sin? And since I am telling you the truth, why don't you believe Me?" (John 8:46).

He [Jesus] never sinned, nor ever deceived anyone (1 Peter 2:22).

It is an easy matter to establish from the Bible and all religious and historical records that all have sinned, even great men and prophets—except Jesus.

THE REASON FOR THE SINLESSNESS OF JESUS

Jesus said, "I and the Father are one" (John 10:30). Jesus and the Father are one in nature. Since God the Father would never sin, it follows that Jesus would not sin either. For this reason, Jesus is the only person who can say "whatever the Father does, the Son also does" (John 5:19).

Jesus always did the absolute will of God and did not do anything on His own accord as Jesus said, "I always do what pleases Him" (John 8:29).

Jesus was able to do God's will and not commit any sin throughout His earthly life because he was not conceived by the natural joining of a man and woman, but rather, by the Holy Spirit. Therefore, He did not inherit the sin nature that has been passed down from Adam to his descendants. This is why Jesus is the only man in human history who lived a sinless life—because He is divine.

Jesus was able to live his life without committing one single sin because his nature is pure and sinless. Since only God can exist without sinning, it is easy to see that Jesus is God manifested in human form.

JESUS CLEANSES US FROM ALL OUR SINS

Jesus is not only sinless, he also cleanses others from their sins (1 John 1:7). Throughout His ministry, Jesus demonstrated His authority to do so. For example, in Mark 2:1-12 Jesus forgave the paralytic of his sins and then healed him. And in Matthew 9:6, Jesus Himself declared that He had the power on earth to forgive sins.

JESUS HAS POWER OVER DEATH

The ability to raise the dead is another power that belongs only to God, yet the Bible records several instances where Jesus demonstrated this ability. For example, when a close friend of Jesus named Lazarus died, Jesus declared to Lazarus' sister, Martha, "I am the resurrection and the life. Anyone who believes in Me will live, even after dying" (John 11:25). Then Jesus raised Lazarus from the dead.

Jesus came to conquer death and give eternal life to whoever believes in Him. Jesus clarified this when He said,

> For just as the Father raises the dead and gives them life, even so the Son gives life to whom He is pleased to give it (John 5:21).

JESUS IS THE INTERCESSOR

The gospel assures us that Jesus is continually interceding for His followers (believers) before God the Father "because Jesus lives forever . . . He is able to save completely those who come to God through Him, because He always lives to intercede for them" (Hebrews 7:24-25).

11

God's Passionate Love for You Compelled Him to Come

God chose to enter our world through Jesus who was conceived by the Holy Spirit in the body of a virgin. He could do this because God is an infinite Spirit. He is One and His oneness is compound. Within the Divine Unity there are three eternal persons of one divine nature who share the same self-existing essence; they are called the Father, the Son, and the Holy Spirit.

Jesus is united with God the Father in one Spirit from all eternity. He took an additional nature, a human nature, and came to earth as God's Ambassador subject to God's authority and dwelt among us as a man.

GOD IS BOTH ALMIGHTY AND HUMBLE

When Jesus lived on earth, He ate, drank, and slept like any other man. Some people ask, "How can Jesus be

God, since God does not need to do the same activities that humans do?"

It is true that God does not have to do any of these human activities, just like a king does not have to sleep where his servants sleep or eat where his servants eat. He certainly does not have to go through such humbling experiences. However, he can choose to do so if he wants to get close to his servants, to experience their feelings, and ultimately solve their problems. He can choose to spend time with them in their environment.

Likewise, the God of the Bible is the Servant-King. The Bible states, "You know the generous grace of our Lord Jesus Christ. Though He was rich, yet for your sakes He became poor, so that by his poverty he could make you rich" (2 Corinthians 8:9).

Please allow me to share with you another story: Before one Labor Day holiday, the President of the United States spent several hours wearing a factory uniform as he talked with and labored alongside hard-working steel manufacturers. He really did put in an honest-day's work and by the end of the shift, his clothes were dirty and smelly. The President was not less honorable because of what he did that day. On the contrary, his humble spirit and actions honored the factory workers and every worker in America—even America itself.

GOD DESIRES TO ASSOCIATE CLOSELY WITH PEOPLE

God reveals Himself as a God of love who desires to meet us at our level and identify with us closely. He longs for us to come to Him so He can embrace us and communicate with us through His Spirit whom He will send to dwell within us. He wants to adopt us as children and become our loving, heavenly Father.

GOD IS ALMIGHTY AND PRESENT EVERYWHERE

We learned from the Bible that God walked in the Garden of Eden and personally communicated with Adam (Genesis 3:8). This did not confine God because He is almighty and ever-present. In the same way, God's incarnation (coming in the form of a man) at a specific time and place did not confine Him either. He remains the almighty, sovereign God who fills the whole universe with His presence and yet desires to reveal Himself to us and fellowship with us one-on-one.

Shall we dare to place boundaries upon God's power and will? Do we not limit God by saying He is unable to express Himself in human form? Man could not become almighty God, but God certainly could come into our world in the form of a man and manifest Himself through the perfect man, Jesus Christ.

GOD DESIRES TO RELATE TO US PERSONALLY

Ultimately, God can only be known through His self-revelations. The Bible declares that God came to us through the person of Jesus Christ, taking on human nature to reveal the infinite in a language the finite can understand.

Please consider this hypothetical situation: If you desired to communicate with a bird and you had unlimited power and authority, what would be the best way for you to do so? Yes, you would become a bird. Then you could communicate on the same level.

Consider another illustration: During the Vietnam War, a certain family was separated. While the wife and two boys were able to move to the United States, the father was forced to stay in Vietnam. For many years they communicated with each other only through letters and pictures. The father could watch his boys grow up only from a distance. Finally, the governments of Vietnam and the United States signed an agreement allowing the father to go to the U.S. to be with his family.

What if the father had said to his family, "I don't really see any need to visit you in person. Communicating through letters and pictures will continue to be sufficient for me." What would you think of such a father? Likewise, what would you think of a God who was able to communicate with and visit His creation in person but refused to do so?

GOD'S DIVINE NATURE IS NEVER DIMINISHED

My dear reader, almighty God was able to appear in the person of Jesus and to personally relate to mankind without staining His divine character.

Jesus' life on earth was a perfect demonstration of God's love, forgiveness, holiness, healing, and salvation. He did not lose His divine nature when He became a man. He raised the dead, healed the lepers, and gave sight to the blind. He manifested many divine characteristics that cannot be attributed to a mere human being. But at the same time, Jesus' humanity was obvious. He walked and talked with His disciples and others. He suffered physical pain. He was fully human.

THE DEITY OF JESUS

Scripture contains many statements confirming the deity of Jesus. It declares that Jesus is:

- Eternal (Everlasting)—He existed before the world was formed (John 8:58; 17:5).

- Ever-Present—He is present everywhere at all times (Matthew 18:20).

- All-Powerful—He demonstrated unlimited, supernatural power and authority (Matthew 8:23-27).

In His divine nature, Jesus is an infinite eternal Spirit. This same divine Being became personally united with human nature and yet retained His divinity. God entered

His creation in a new way and experienced it while still remaining God. He did not only walk among us; He became one of us—in a true human form.

Man Was Created in God's Image

My dear friend, God chose to save us. He accomplished this goal by appearing in the form of a perfect, sinless man to be our personal Savior. God did not become incarnate in a plant, bird, or animal because they do not bear His image. But we know from the Bible that God created us in His image. God said, "Let Us make human beings in Our image" (Genesis 1:26).

Bible scholar, Bedru Kateregga, explains that

man created in the image of God does not mean that God looks like man or that man looks like God. But it does mean that man has profound Godlike qualities. . . .[1]

For example, God created man with the ability to be loving, just, and compassionate and most of us strive to become more loving, caring, and overall better people. . . .This desire in ourselves is the witness of our God—likeness within our conscience. It's a persistent voice in the conscience that we should become better people, that we do not always do what we know we should do, that we really should be more kind, true, reliable, pure, more Godlike.[2]

It is also Godlike to be humble and to love sacrificially.

JESUS IS THE PERFECT MEDIATOR

Jesus is the perfect Mediator between God and man. The Bible declares, "This is good and pleases God our Savior, who wants everyone to be saved and to understand the truth. For there is only one God and one Mediator who can reconcile God and humanity—The man Christ Jesus. He gave his life to purchase freedom for everyone" (1 Timothy 2:3-6). Only Christ could be called the perfect and acceptable sacrifice to God. In Him we see all the necessary characteristics that must be found in the Mediator (Savior).

THE SAVIOR MUST BE HUMAN

How could God—who is Spirit—pay the penalty for the sins of man who is flesh? It was a human penalty He wanted to bear; therefore, Jesus Christ acquired human form, became a true member of the human race, and paid the penalty. As a man, Christ could represent humanity.

By the way, Jesus understands our struggles because He faced them as a human being on earth.

THE SAVIOR MUST BE DIVINE

To take away the sins of the world, the Savior had to pay the full price. Therefore, the sacrifice had to have an infinite value.

Everything Jesus did derived unique significance from His divine identity. The Savior descended to us from God so He could lift us up to God.

The Savior Unites You with God

Since Jesus shares the very nature of God: "For in Christ lives all the fullness of God in a human body" (Colossians 2:9);

and because Jesus said, "I am . . . the life" (John 14:6);

and because He also promised, "Here I am! I stand at the door [of your heart] and knock. If anyone hears My voice and opens the door, I will come in" (Revelation 3:20);

therefore, the moment you believe in who Jesus is and invite Him to enter your life, Jesus will enter your life through His spirit and give you the abundant, rich life God created you to enjoy. You will be full of life; you will feel more alive than ever. God guarantees this.

Jesus alone qualified as the connecting link between God and man. The gulf between heaven and earth was bridged by the coming of Jesus. None but Jesus Christ could give spiritual and eternal life to all those who believe in Him.

God wants to be united to you to share with you all He has.

The awesome truth is that the moment you believe in Jesus, you become united to God. Jesus prayed, "I pray also for those who will believe in Me. . . . Father, just as You are in Me and I am in You. May they also be in Us . . . I in them and You in Me" (John 17:20-23). A marvelous transformation and inheritance awaits those who believe in Jesus. Your future will be awesome.

The union of Godhead and manhood—in the person of Jesus—made it possible for man and God to be united forever.

Jesus Submitted to the Father's Will

While living on earth, Jesus voluntarily took "the very nature of a servant" (Philippians 2). Christ only used His divine power to serve the Father and act according to His will. This reminds me of a wonderful story:

There was once a noble king whose kingdom was invaded by a distant enemy. The enemy captured many of the king's people and used them as slaves in a remote land. The king devised a plan to free his people. As part of that plan, the king asked his only son, the prince, to become a prisoner as well. The prince agreed and set off to become enslaved among his people. He lived with them and became one of them, wearing their clothes, eating their food, and suffering the same treatment they suffered. Then at the right time, the prince used his power and influence to set his people free from the captivity of the enemy. The son restored the honor of his father and his kingdom.

Likewise, Jesus set us free and restored the Father's kingdom to us. Again, the Bible confirms that "though He [Jesus} was rich, yet for your sakes He became poor, so that you through His poverty might become rich" (2 Corinthians 8:9).

God's Amazing Grace Toward Us

Forgiving sins (receiving salvation) is accomplished only by God, for no person is able to earn it by following rules, rituals, or doing good works.

Imagine you're drowning at sea; you can barely keep your head above the water. What would be your most urgent need—someone to give you swimming instructions and ask you to try harder? Of course not. You need someone powerful enough to dive into the water and rescue you. In the Bible, God tells us that everyone is sinking in the depths of sin and God personally came to rescue us.

Awesome Wonder of the Incarnation

The incarnation of Christ, God taking an additional (human) nature, leads us to an awesome wonder: "Great is the mystery of godliness: God was manifested in the flesh" (1 Timothy 3:16). What a wonder! The eternal One entered time, became a man, and walked among us!

Before you read further, please stop and say a prayer. Ask God to guide you to His truth, to an understanding of His Word.

12

⤜∾⤛

God's Unspeakable Love Manifested through Jesus' Death and Resurrection

We can trust the Bible and what it says about Jesus' crucifixion because it records the testimony of eyewitnesses about events that took place publicly and privately. For example, seven weeks after Jesus' crucifixion, Peter said to a great multitude of Jews:

> Men of Israel, listen to this: Jesus of Nazareth was a man accredited by God to you by miracles, wonders and signs which God did among you through Him, as you yourselves know. This man was handed over to you by God's set purpose and foreknowledge; and you, with the help of wicked men, put Him to death by nailing Him to the cross. But God raised Him from the dead, freeing Him from the agony of death, because it was impossible for death to keep its hold on Him (Acts 2: 22–24).

After Peter said these words to the crowd of Jews, they did not deny that they crucified Jesus; instead, the Bible records that 3,000 people put their faith in Jesus.

Jesus even predicted to His twelve disciples His own death and resurrection:

> Jesus took the twelve aside and told them, "We are going up to Jerusalem, and everything that is written by the prophets about the Son of Man will be fulfilled. He will be handed over to the Gentiles. They will mock Him, insult Him, spit on Him, flog Him and kill Him. On the third day He will rise again" (Luke 18:31-33 and Matthew 16:21).

OLD TESTAMENT PROPHECIES REGARDING THE CRUCIFIXION OF JESUS

The Old Testament was written hundreds of years before Jesus' crucifixion and contains astounding prophecies. Two of these amazing and specific prophecies are found in Isaiah 53 and Psalm 22. Let's take a closer look at them:

THE DEATH AND BURIAL OF JESUS

Isaiah 53:9 gives specific details about the death of Jesus hundreds of years before He was born: "He was assigned a grave with the wicked, and with the rich in his death." No one at the time of the prophet Isaiah could understand the meaning of these words. At face value, the account of His burial appears to be a contradiction.

Was Jesus buried with the outcasts or was He buried with the noble and rich? Both seemingly conflicting statements came to pass:

According to Roman law, criminals that were crucified were supposed to be thrown into a burning pit and cremated. However, this did not happen to Jesus. Instead, Jesus was buried in the tomb of a rich man. Matthew 27:57-60 reads:

> As evening approached, there came a rich man from Arimathea, named Joseph, who had himself become a disciple of Jesus. Going to Pilate, he asked for Jesus' body, and Pilate ordered that it be given to him. Joseph took the body, wrapped it in a clean linen cloth, and placed it in his own new tomb that he had cut out of the rock.

By being crucified with thieves and buried in the tomb of a rich man, Jesus was assigned a grave with both the wicked and the rich. Thus, what seemed an unexplained paradox in Isaiah 53 was easily understood when Jesus fulfilled the entire prophecy upon his death and burial.

THE DIVIDING OF CHRIST'S CLOTHES

Other prophetic words of Christ's crucifixion are found in Psalm 22:18: "They divide my garments among them and cast lots for my clothing." This verse was a mystery to the people at that time and seemed to contain another contradiction. Did they take the clothes and divide them among themselves, or did they cast lots to see who would get them? Which one was it?

Let's examine the course of events: When the soldiers crucified Jesus, they took His clothes and divided them into four shares, one for each of them. This fulfilled the first part of the prophecy: "They divide my garments among them."

But the undergarment remained. It was seamless and woven in one piece from top to bottom. The soldiers said to one another, "Let's not tear it, let's decide by lot who will get it." By doing this, the soldiers fulfilled the second part of the prophecy that said, "They . . . cast lots for my clothing." And that is what the soldiers did. The prophecy of Psalm 22:18 was explained and fulfilled to the letter at the foot of the cross. This event is documented in John 19:23-24.

Incidentally, the Jews in the first century who rejected Jesus as their Savior dared not delete from their sacred Scripture any of the numerous Messianic prophecies that were fulfilled by Jesus. They remain today as evidence that Jesus is the predicted Messiah.

JESUS CAME BACK FROM THE DEAD

Jesus did not stay in the tomb.

The angel said to the women, "Do not be afraid, for I know that you are looking for Jesus, who was crucified. He is not here; He has risen, just as He said. Come and see the place where He lay. Then go quickly and tell His disciples: He has risen from the dead and is going ahead of you into Galilee. There you will see Him. Now I have told you" (Matthew 28:5-7).

When you read John 20, you will learn that eyewitnesses saw Jesus' tomb empty. You can also read the eyewitness testimony of the apostle Peter recorded in Acts 10:34-43.

The apostles and others would not have proclaimed the resurrection of Jesus throughout Jerusalem if the emptiness of the tomb had not first been established. But there is much more to the resurrection account than an empty tomb.

JESUS APPEARED TO HIS DISCIPLES

Jesus' disciples believed in His resurrection because they actually saw Him alive after dying by crucifixion. We read, "When the disciples were together with the doors locked for fear of the Jews, Jesus came and stood among them and said, 'Peace be with you.' After He said this, He showed them His hands and side. The disciples were overjoyed when they saw the Lord" (John 20:19-20).

Jesus also personally appeared to Thomas (who had doubted that Jesus really did rise from the dead) and said to him, "Put your finger here: see My hands. Reach out your hand and put it into My side. Stop doubting and believe" (John 20:27).

Because Thomas saw and touched the physically resurrected Christ, he was inspired and compelled to preach the gospel even as far away as India. It is recorded that wherever he went, he spoke about Jesus' death and resurrection. Thomas became a martyr because of the resurrection message he so boldly proclaimed.

Hundreds of other witnesses saw the risen Christ over a forty-day period in various locations and at various times. For example, Jesus was seen in His resurrected body by over 500 brethren at once (1 Corinthians 15:1-6). You can read more accounts of Jesus' resurrection in John 21:1-23, Mark 16:9-13, and Acts 1:3.

THE HOLY SCRIPTURES FORETOLD JESUS' RESURRECTION

Hundreds of years before the birth of Jesus Christ, God inspired King David to predict the resurrection of Christ: "Therefore my heart is glad and my tongue rejoices; my body also will rest secure, because you will not abandon me to the grave, nor will you let your Holy One see decay" (Psalm 16:9-10).

The apostle Peter explained to the Jews how this prophecy was fulfilled in the resurrection of Jesus:

> Men of Israel, listen to this: Jesus of Nazareth was a man accredited by God to you by miracles, wonders and signs, which God did among you through Him,

as you yourselves know. This man was handed over to you by God's set purpose and foreknowledge; and you, with the help of wicked men, put Him to death by nailing Him to the cross. But God raised Him from the dead, freeing Him from the agony of death, because it was impossible for death to keep its hold on Him. David said about Him: "Because you will not abandon me to the grave, nor will you let your Holy One see decay. . . . " Brothers, I can tell you confidently that the patriarch David died and was buried, and his tomb is here to this day. But he was a prophet . . . Seeing what was ahead, he spoke of the resurrection of the Christ, that He was not abandoned to the grave, nor did His body see decay. God has raised this Jesus to life, and we are all witnesses of the fact (Acts 2:22-32).

It is obvious in his words, that Peter was absolutely positive that the tomb was empty and that Jesus rose to life again.

Two Credible Professors Speak Out on Historical Evidence

Several renowned historians have studied the resurrection account and have concluded that the evidence in support of the event is undeniable. One such scholar is Professor Thomas Arnold, the Lord Master of Rugby University, the author of *The History of Rome,* and the Chair of Modern History at Oxford University. After carefully sifting through the ancient documentation on the crucifixion and resurrection of Christ, this esteemed, modern-day scholar wrote:

> I have been used for many years to study the histories of other times and to examine and weigh the evidence of those who have written about them. I know of no one fact in the history of mankind which is proven by better and fuller evidence of every sort, to the understanding of a fair inquirer, than the great sign which God has given us that Christ died and rose again from the dead.[1]

Another scholar was John Singleton Copley, a professor at Cambridge University and Attorney General of Great Britain in 1824. He rose to the highest office as a judge in England and was recognized as one of the greatest legal minds in British history. After his death, a document was found among his private papers in which he had written, "I know pretty well what evidence is and I tell you, such evidence as that for the resurrection has never been broken down yet."[2]

UNDISPUTED FACTS OF THE RESURRECTION

Certain facts are accepted as historically accurate even by nonreligious historians. They include:

- Jesus Christ was crucified and died.
- Jesus' tomb was empty after His burial.
- There was a proclamation that Jesus had risen.

The Gospel fills in the details. According to the Gospel, after Jesus Christ died by crucifixion, His body was taken down from the cross and laid in the tomb of Joseph of Arimathea. A large stone weighing between one and two tons was placed at the front of the tomb, and the Roman seal was placed on that stone. Well-trained Roman guards constantly watched and guarded the tomb. On the third day, the tomb was empty.

Following Jesus' arrest, His disciples were afraid. We read, "Then all the disciples deserted Him and fled" (Matthew 26:56). However, several days after the resurrection, this same group of fearful followers courageously proclaimed the resurrection of Jesus. The sudden transformation occurred not only because they had seen an empty tomb but because they had seen and experienced the risen Christ.

CREDIBILITY OF JESUS' DISCIPLES

If someone were to ask, "Did the disciples lie about seeing Jesus alive again?" The answer would be simple. What could they possibly have gained by lying? Prestige? Wealth?

According to recorded tradition, Jude and Peter were crucified, Luke was hanged from an olive tree, Paul was beheaded, Philip was scourged and crucified, James (the son of Zebedee) was killed by the sword, Mark was dragged through the streets by his feet and then burned alive, James and Barnabas were stoned to death. This treatment was their earthly "reward" for proclaiming the good news that Jesus is risen, He is alive, He offers forgiveness of sins, and He gives eternal life to those who believe in Him.

Would these disciples subject themselves to such cruel punishment if Jesus did not rise from the dead? Let me answer that with this observation. When I was a lawyer in Egypt. I worked for my father who has practiced law for about fifty years. Likewise, my grandfather was a lawyer for about fifty years, and my older brother is currently a judge in the highest court in Egypt. Most of my extended family are in the legal profession. We have never seen or heard of a witness who allowed himself to go to prison or to suffer for something he knew was a lie.

THE ASCENSION OF JESUS

The ascension of Jesus into heaven is clearly recorded in the Bible. Mark 16:19 reads: "After the Lord Jesus had spoken to them [His apostles], He was taken up into heaven." Luke 24:49-53 and Acts 1:9-11 also record this momentous event.

Jesus is the eternal Son of God, and heaven is His permanent home. Therefore, it was impossible for Jesus, after He accomplished His mission on earth, to return to dust like all other prophets naturally do. Jesus told us His mission:

For I have come down from heaven to do the will of God who sent Me, not to do my own will (John 6:38).

Jesus Christ fulfilled His mission, returned to heaven, and is without a doubt higher than all creation. He is alive with the heavenly Father today!

13

God's Amazing Love:
He Is Coming Back for You

Jesus is coming back for His followers. This is prophesied in the Old Testament (Daniel 7:13-14) and confirmed in the New Testament: "At that time men will see the Son of Man coming in clouds with great power and glory" (Mark 13:26).

JESUS WILL GIVE US GLORIFIED BODIES

When Jesus comes back, He will transform His true followers (true believers) into His image, to share His glory with them forever. We read about this glorious promise in the New Testament:

> We are citizens of heaven, where the Lord Jesus Christ lives. And we are eagerly waiting for him to return as our Savior. He will take our weak mortal

bodies and change them into glorious bodies like his own (Philippians 3:20-21).

It is so exciting to know that Jesus will give us new, glorified bodies suited for heaven. At Jesus' first coming, He made Himself like us; at Jesus' second coming, He will make us like Him. We read:

> We know that when He appears, we shall be like Him, for we shall see Him as He is (1 John 3:2).

> Just as we are now like the earthly man [Adam], we will someday be like the heavenly man [Jesus] (1 Corinthians 15:49).

JESUS WILL TAKE BELIEVERS TO HEAVEN

Part of the wonderful news of the Bible is that when Jesus descends from heaven, He will gather all people who believe in Him; then we will join Him "and so we will be with the Lord forever" (1 Thessalonians 4:17).

We look forward to this awesome day when we will be with Jesus as He promised us:

> Don't let your hearts be troubled. Trust in God, and trust also in me. There is more than enough room in my Father's home. If this were not so, would I have told you that I am going to prepare a place for you? When everything is ready, I will come and get you, so that you will always be with me where I am (John 14:1-3).

JESUS IS COMING TO JUDGE THE WORLD

The Bible teaches that the Son of God, by coming in the likeness of man, has revealed God to men and has brought men face to face with God. He shall return to judge the earth. Jesus Himself declares:

> The Father judges no one. Instead, he has given the Son absolute authority to judge, so that everyone will honor the Son just as they honor the Father (John 5:22-23).

Jesus will be the most glorious sight that humans have ever seen. The suffering Servant will come back as the conquering King. He will put an end to evil and will rule with holy justice.

❦

THE UNIQUENESS OF JESUS LEADS TO A CONCLUSION

God expects us to sincerely evaluate and accept the truth that He reveals to us.

The Bible attributes characteristics to Jesus that only belong to God. The unique features of Jesus' life prove that He is more than a mere prophet. The prophets we have heard or read about were ordinary men. Each one was born of a father and a mother. They lived normal lives. Sometimes they did good things and other times they sinned against God and against fellow human beings. When their lives ended, they returned to the dust from where they came.

Jesus' virgin birth tells us that God made the only exception to the natural process of procreation in having Jesus conceived by the power of God's Spirit. Jesus was also unique in His sinlessness, His ability to raise the dead, perform the greatest miracles, His ascension, and His inevitable return to judge the world. Thus, His abilities and traits compel the conclusion that Jesus is the unique, eternal Son of God who came to save us.

Jesus was born and raised in a small village and worked as a carpenter until He was thirty years old. He never had a position in government. He at no time owned a house. He never had an army. He never fought a war or commanded His disciples to fight. He had ministered for only three-and-a-half years before His enemies arrested and crucified Him. Jesus' entire life was an accumulation of acts of love.

There has never been a prophet, military leader, educator, or king who has made a more positive impact on humanity than Jesus. Jesus Christ is superior to all others in His moral influence and in His promotion of human happiness and well-being.

Jesus was unique and superior in His teaching. For example, He taught:

Love your enemies (Matthew 5:44).

Love your neighbor as yourself (Matthew 22:39).

Do to others as you would like them to do to you (Luke 6:31).

Jesus taught us to serve one another. For example, when He washed and dried the feet of His disciples He said to them, "I have given you an example to follow. Do as I have done to you" (John 13:15).

If you read Jesus' teachings recorded in the Bible, you will discover that if people only obeyed what Jesus taught, all the problems in the world would be solved.

Two thousand years have passed since the death of Jesus. He is still the most loved and honored Person who ever walked on this earth because he loved and lived supernaturally.

14

∽

God Sent Jesus to Save You

Sin is an integral part of our human nature. All kinds of iniquity dwell in the human heart, such as lust, envy, jealousy, greed, pride, and selfishness. These sins and others have vicious control within each person; they make all humans captive to their power and ongoing temptations.

JESUS WON THE BATTLE AGAINST SIN

Jesus, the only One who is pure from sin, came "in the likeness of sinful man" and "He condemned sin in sinful man [in the flesh]" (Romans 8:3).

The awesome news of the gospel is that Jesus defeated the power of sin in its own dwelling place—inside the human body. His divine nature enabled Him to live as a man without committing one single sin; in this way, He won the battle over the temptations of Satan and sin on our behalf.

We Can Be Free from the Power of Sin

The wonderful news of the gospel is that God made it possible for you to be united with Jesus through His Spirit, who will live within you at the very moment you place your faith in Jesus as your Savior. As a natural consequence of being united with Jesus, you will enjoy the fruits of His victory. At that moment, you can experience freedom from the bondage to sin.

Jesus said, "I tell you the truth, everyone who sins is a slave to sin." He also said, "If the Son sets you free, you will be free indeed" (John 8:34, 36).

The gospel's beautiful message is that Jesus came to save you and set you free from the captivity and love of sin. The Savior, Jesus Christ, came to do what the law and the prophets could not do: "The reason the Son of God appeared was to destroy the Devil's work" (1 John 3:8).

Physicians can cure many physical illnesses, but only Jesus can heal sinners, set them free from doing wrong, and make them righteous. Jesus can give you the ability to do the right thing.

Jesus warns us, "Unless you believe that I Am who I claim to be, you will die in your sins" (John 8:24).

You Can Be Saved from the Penalty of Sin

Jesus suffered the most horrible consequence of our sin—death. By suffering the wrath of God toward sin, Jesus paid for the sin (debt) of every person.

Because believers in Christ are united with Him, they share in and benefit from Christ's death and resurrection: "Since we have been united with him in his death, we will also be raised to life as he was" (Romans 6:5).

The good news of the Bible is that Jesus came to save you and me and set us free from having to suffer the consequences of everything wrong we did.

You Can Enjoy God's Forgiveness

When you believe that the penalty for everything you did wrong is already paid for through Christ, you will be united to Christ and experience the forgiveness of God for all your sins.

In other words, since Christ already paid the penalty, and you are united with Him, you will benefit from what He did for you on the cross. Jesus also will set you free from any guilty feelings or thoughts that exist within you as a consequence of the wrong things you did. You will then enjoy a wonderful peace with God and peace within yourself.

You Can Live Forever with God

When Jesus rose from the dead and ascended to be with God the Father, He declared victory over death. He reversed the worst consequence of sin, which is eternal separation from God's presence. Christ's resurrection is the first in a long line of resurrections to come of those who believe in Him. True believers in Christ only die physically and then will enjoy eternal life with God forever.

YOU CAN BE CERTAIN THAT YOU ARE GOING TO HEAVEN

You can be certain within your soul and mind that you are going to heaven. The moment you believe in Jesus and go to God in repentance, God's Holy Spirit will come to dwell within you, and He will assure you that you are now going to heaven. Paradise will become your home and your destiny.

> And Christ lives within you, so even though your body will die because of sin, the Spirit gives you life because you have been made right with God. The Spirit of God, who raised Jesus from the dead, lives in you. And just as God raised Christ Jesus from the dead, he will give life to your mortal bodies by this same Spirit living within you (Romans 8:10-11).

The reason you will know for sure you are going to heaven is that the same Jesus who lives in heaven will come to live in you now through His eternal Spirit. The living and life-giving Spirit of Christ imparts to you eternal life with God. Jesus declares to us, "Because I live, you also will live" (John 14:19).

JESUS BRIDGED THE GAP

Jesus fully bridged the gap between heaven and earth. He made it possible for sinful man to be reconciled with the holy God. He declared, "I am the way and the truth and the life. No one comes to the Father except through Me" (John 14:6).

JESUS SATISFIES OUR SPIRITUAL THIRST

Jesus knows you need a genuine friend and He wants to be that friend (John 15:14-15). Just imagine what it would be like to have a perfect friend who is able to do everything good for you. Jesus said, "My purpose is to give them a rich and satisfying life" (John 10:10). God created us in such a way that we will never be satisfied or enjoy life fully until we have the right relationship with Him through faith in Jesus.

Jesus also satisfies our deepest spiritual and emotional longing. He said,

I am the bread of life. He who comes to Me will never go hungry, and he who believes in Me will never be thirsty (John 6:35).

Jesus knows that your soul is like a traveller wandering through the desert of life. You are hungry for love and peace, thirsty for joy and happiness, and are looking for it everywhere without success. Christ promises you that if you go to Him, this deep longing will be satisfied.

When you believe in Christ, He will be like "cold water" to your thirsty soul.

God is inviting you to a life of joy despite any adverse circumstances you may face. Jesus said, "I have told you these things so that you will be filled with my joy. Yes, your joy will overflow" (John 15:11).

WHAT IS YOUR DECISION?

Jesus speaks to you because He loves you. Jesus promised, "Come to me, all of you who are weary and carry heavy burdens, and I will give you rest" (Matthew 11:28).

Jesus wants to guide you and help you discover the purpose of your life. He said, "I am the light of the world. If you follow me, you won't have to walk in darkness, because you will have the light that leads to life" (John 8:12). Jesus would like to remove the darkness, error, and confusion from your mind.

Jesus offers eternal life with God to you and to me:

Most assuredly, I say to you, he who believes in Me has everlasting life (John 6:47).

When you believe Jesus' words and obey God by faith, you will sing and jump for joy.

GOD'S SUPREME LOVE DRAWS US TO HIM

My dear friend, I urge you to believe God's Word and take a step of faith. I know from personal experience that the moment you believe in Jesus as your Lord and Savior, you, too, will actually experience and taste within your heart and soul God's great and wonderful love for you. God wants to make you satisfied. He desires to fill your life with joy, love, living hope, and peace. God desires to have fellowship with you. God is speaking to you right now saying, "I have loved you, my people, with an everlasting love. With unfailing love I have drawn you to myself" (Jeremiah 31:3).

Jesus declares, "For God so loved the world that He gave His one and only Son, that whoever believes in Him shall not perish but have eternal life" (John 3:16).

For God	*the greatest Lover*
so loved	*the greatest degree*
the world	*the greatest company*
that He gave	*the greatest act*
His one and only Son	*the greatest gift (Jesus)*
that whoever	*the greatest opportunity*
believes	*the greatest simplicity*
in Him	*the greatest attraction*
should not perish	*the greatest promise*
but	*the greatest difference*
have	*the greatest certainty*
everlasting life	*the greatest possession.*

My friend, our loving God is longing to have a personal relationship with you. He chose you—now the choice is yours to make.

Your joy now and eternal happiness depends on your decision. If you choose to put your faith in Jesus as your Lord and Savior, here is a suggested personal and specific prayer. Pray it, if you mean it, with all your heart:

Thank you Jesus for dying on the cross to pay the penalty for my sins. I need you to come into my life and be my Savior and Lord.

God, I do not want to live far from you any longer. I am sorry for everything I have done wrong. I ask you to forgive me because of what Jesus has done for me. I want to experience your love and do your will.

In Jesus' name, Amen.

If you prayed this prayer, let me be the first to welcome you into God's eternal family. I would also like to congratulate you on having made the best and most important decision of your life—receiving the miracle of eternal life with God!

Your New Life Walking with God

My dear brother and sister in Christ, now that you are a child of God, please pay attention to these important issues:

First, find a church that faithfully teaches God's Word. Please beware of churches or groups that claim to be "Christian" but do not correctly follow the teachings of the Bible. It is essential to join a church that teaches one must be born-again by the Spirit of God (John 3:3).

Second, it is important to read the Bible daily. It is the complete, inspired, and reliable Word of God. And remember to spend time in God's presence, in prayer so that you will grow spiritually. Talk to God anytime—He is your perfect, loving, heavenly Father and best Friend.

Third, while we are on this earth, we will all face difficulties and hard times. However, God promises He will be with us and He will cause all things to work together for our good because we love Him (Romans 8:28).

My friend, now you begin your journey of discovering and experiencing the fruitful, meaningful, and rich life that God created for you. By walking with God daily, through faith, you will experience His awesome promises for you, and you will be able to enjoy the wonderful blessings God has for you.

BIBLIOGRAPHY

Bruce, F.F., The New Testament Documents: Are They Reliable? InterVarsity Press, Downers Grove, IL (2000).

Crawford, Craig, *The Prophecies: A Journey to the End of Time.* Prophecy Press (1999).

Geisler, Norman and Nix, William, *From God to Us: How We Got Our Bible.* Moody Press, Chicago (1974).

Halley, Henry, *Halley's Bible Handbook*, Grand Rapids, MI: Zondervan, 2007.

Kateregga, Badru Dan & Shenk, David W, *A Muslim and a Christian in Dialogue.* Herald Press, PA (1997).

Lockyer, Herbert, *All the Messianic Prophecies of the Bible.* Zondervan Publishing House, Grand Rapids, MI (1973).

McDowell, Josh, *The New Evidence That Demands a Verdict.* Thomas Nelson Publishers, Nashville, Tennessee (1999).

Morris, Henry M., *Science and the Bible.* Moody Press, Chicago (1986).

Smith, Wilbur M., *Therefore Stand: Christian Apologetics.* Baker Book House, Grand Rapids, MI (1965).

Walvoord, John F., *Every Prophecy of the Bible.* Cook Communications, Colorado Springs, CO (1999).

FOOTNOTES

CHAPTER FOUR:

1. See Bibliography (McDowell).
2. See Bibliography (Morris).
3. See Bibliography (Walvoord).
4. Geisler and Nix, *From God to Us: How We Got Our Bible*, p 139.
5. See Bibliography (Bruce, Geisler and Nix).
6. Halley, Henry, *Halley's Bible Handbook*, pp 1092-1101.

CHAPTER NINE:

1. See Bibliography (Lockyer).

CHAPTER ELEVEN:

1. Kateregga and Shenk, *Islam and Christianity*, p 19.
2. Ibid, pp 97-98.

CHAPTER TWELVE:

1. McDowell, Josh, *The New Evidence That Demands a Verdict*, pp 216-217.
2. See Bibliography (Smith) pp 425-426.

ACKNOWLEDGMENTS

Words cannot express my gratitude to my loving heavenly Father for guiding and enabling me to serve Him through the writing of this book.

To my beloved wife, Hala, I pray that I will love you in the most deepest way possible all the days of our lives. Thank you for loving me and supporting me since I met you. You are the best and most wonderful human being and friend I know. I love you.

I am so grateful to Randy Vannoy for spending so many hours graciously assisting me technically in the preparation of the final manuscript of this book.

I thank God always for my financial and prayer partners. God used them so richly to enable me to communicate the message of God's love and salvation effectively to multitudes of people.

For more information visit

GladNewsMinistry.com

or call

714-514-2558